THIS IS FOR REAL

This Is
For Real

George Bates

with
Noel Davidson

Christian Year Publications

ISBN-13: 978 1 872734 46 0

Permission kindly granted by Mr Noel Davidson, holder of the copyright.

Typeset by John Ritchie Ltd., Kilmarnock
Printed by Bell & Bain Ltd., Glasgow

Contents

Introduction

"Do you know George Bates?" came the question. From the other end of the telephone.

I thought for a moment.

"Well, I have heard him preach once or twice," I replied. "But to say....No. I wouldn't say that I know him."

That was to change. The preliminary question was a lead-in to the request from the publisher that I write a book. This book. The story of the life and spiritual experiences of George Bates.

Over the past year I have met George many times. We have talked together for hours on end. Dined together. Walked for miles through forests together. But more important than all of those, we have prayed together.

People have asked me, during the past year, since they have heard that I have had frequent sharing-sessions with him, "What is there about George Bates that makes people flock to hear him?" or, "Why is it that so many people are moved by his preaching?"

I would not have known the answer to that type of query a year ago. But I know it now. It is simple. It is one word. Prayer.

When George prays he touches heaven. Every time and straight away. He lives in close, direct contact with God. It is evident that when he prays, his God is at his elbow. Literally "only a prayer away".

There's just one useful, practical discovery that I have made, however, in relation to his harmony with Heaven. It is unwise to ask George to give thanks for a hot meal. He has so much to say to God, even about potatoes, that it will be cooled before you get eating it!

He thinks nothing of spending days in prayer and fasting. Or spending entire nights in prayer.

And God has blessed him. And blesses his ministry.

But to write it all down! All the encounters with God he has had in his lifetime! Proved well-nigh impossible.

George would say, "We must weave in a wee bit about..." or "We really should mention the time when.... "

On many occasions we have had to put the brakes on. Often I found myself saying to him, "Hold on there a minute, George. People aren't going to want your life-story in ten volumes. In hardback. They will only be looking for the one book. And probably a paperback at that!"

So as you read this book you will be sharing in the most moving events in a young man's life. His search after God. His craving for satisfaction. And truth. And reality.

And the end of the search.

The Ultimate. The Only Solution.

God's power and provision in his life. For himself, his wife and family.

"Do you know George Bates?" was the question.

"Yes," I can answer, truthfully, now. "I know him well."

But much more significantly, over a constant twelve-month contact with him, I have come to know his God, and mine, even better.

May this be your experience.

It will be great if you enjoy this book. And marvel at the many and mighty Divine interventions in George's life.

But may it go further than that. When you finish the very last chapter, and close the book, and even before you get the chance to recommend it to someone else for their enjoyment, may it have so touched your life that you will say, "Isn't God wonderful? I would love to come to know Him in a real, deep, genuine way. Just like that."

It is possible. George is the proof.

CHAPTER 1

The Magic Lantern

"I'll tell you, shall I
Something I remember?
Something that still means
A great deal to me.
It was long ago."
E. Farjeon.

People love to look back. They love to remember. They love to think of sun-baked play-days in the street where they lived, or of the glorious summer days wandering through the fields of the farm where they grew up.

When they meet their childhood friends they enjoy recalling those days.

"Do you remember the night...or the day...or the time...or the week...?" they ask.

On looking back the days appeared endlessly sunny and the people were usually kind.

Childhood memories are fascinating, aren't they?

George Bates was born in East Belfast just at the start of the Second World War. October 1939.

If he were asked for his childhood recollections of those exciting growing-up-in-Belfast-days, what would he say? What was the most memorable event of his childhood? What would it be?

His brother Roy was born when George was three years old, and his sister Moira came some years later. His brother and sister and he were very close, great pals, but they weren't involved in the event that George recounts as the most important memory of those childhood days.

Perhaps it would be 8th June, 1946. On that morning George was standing up in front of hundreds of other children in the Assembly Hall of Avoniel Primary School singing lustily,

"Rule Britannia
Britannia rules the waves."

They were gathered to celebrate the end of the war. After the singing each child was presented with a victory document from the King with the inscription:

"FOR SHARING IN THE HARDSHIPS AND DANGERS OF TOTAL WAR"

No. It wasn't that. George had just started in Junior Infants. What would he know about "the hardships and dangers of total war"? What did he care about Hitler?

Maybe it was the day he innocently took his mother's purse. He didn't understand the value of money at that time, as he was so young. Nor did he understand how much his mother needed those few coins and notes -or how hard his father had worked to earn them. All he did know was that it seemed to make him a lot of friends as he distributed them. He just dished them out. Everybody loved him. Everybody crowded around him. And soon all the money was gone.

George remembers the agony of his broken-hearted mother as she tried to retrieve the week's housekeeping allowance. She asked his friends. She asked the parents of his friends. She asked anyone at all she thought would help and she recovered some of it. But not all. That memory will live with George forever. But the most important recollection? No. That wasn't it either.

What was it then? What could it be?

Was it the day he was knocked down on the Avoniel Road? George and his friends used to love to play tig around the air-raid shelters, which weren't much use for anything else. After all, the war was over wasn't it? The young tigplayers often chased each other out of the shelters and across the road.

They usually escaped unscathed.

One day George didn't though.

He was struck by a car and knocked unconscious. Out

cold. He recovered in bed, the centre of attraction, with everyone trying to tell him what he already knew anyway. He could easily have been killed.

George remembers how upset the driver was. Fortunate was it not that the driver was also a caring doctor?

He often wondered afterwards if it was for his benefit that the teacher, on the first day back at school after the holidays told that story. It was a story about someone who was NEARLY KILLED but who lived to eventually serve God in a mighty way.

Close shave that one. Narrow squeak. But the most vivid recollection?

No. Not that either.

What about the night of the magic lantern? Could that rate highly in George's childhood memories?

George and his friends enjoyed themselves together. They played together round the streets. They gazed in the shop windows together. They came and went to school together. In groups they ambled down to Avoniel Primary School and slid in and out through a child-sized gap in the railings. Saved them walking away round to the gate.

One of the great features of this childhood friendship was the chat. The constant talk and discussion, and occasionally even argument. Like the men of Athens in the Bible they loved to hear or to tell some new thing. Something exciting to relieve the tedium of the back-and-forward-to-school-days, the-seven-threes-are-twenty-one, seven-fours-are-twenty-eight days.

Such an exciting thing was the magic lantern. Some of George's friends went up to a little hall at the corner of the street once a week. The "wee meetin" they called it.

George didn't go. He and Roy went shiny-faced, hair-well-brushed, penny-in-hand to Sunday School every Sunday.

George sang, "There is a Green Hill" at Easter.

He sang "Away in a Manger" at Christmas.

He spent the rest of the year thinking up hard questions for the Sunday School teacher to answer.

And that was enough for him.

To go in the middle of the week to a "wee meetin" as well would be a bit too much!

One morning on the way to School his friends were excited. They were all fired-up about next Tuesday.

"George," they said, two or three of them at once. "You must come to the meeting next week. There's a man coming with a magic lantern."

"A magic lantern," retorted George. "What's that?"

No one seemed to be very sure of the exact nature of the magic lantern, but they all knew one thing about it. The same thing.

It was going to be great!

George's imagination ran riot on the magic lantern. He imagined a man in black, sitting at the front, rubbing a lamp until something happened.

Perhaps there would be white billowing smoke, or voices, or pictures in the air.

As the word spread about the magic lantern, information filtered through as well. Somebody's daddy said it was about pictures. You saw nice pictures.

At least, George thought, that cuts out the voices and the smoke. But he decided to go anyway.

It would always be something different.

When the day of the magic lantern came there was very little work done in School.

The excitement was bubbling just below the surface.

"This is the day that the man is coming!" the children were saying to one another.

It was pointless telling anyone that this was the day of the magic lantern. Everybody knew. They had all been talking about it for a week!

George's friends called for him, early, to take him to the wee meeting. It was magic lantern time at last.

George enjoyed the meeting. The singing at the beginning was lively. "Choruses" they called them.

Then came the moment of truth. The magic lantern. This

was what he had talked about, thought about, dreamed about.

The magic lantern turned out to be a small machine with a big light. It projected pictures, pretty pictures, up on to a screen.

It was all a new experience for young George. The magic lantern was new, the pictures on the screen were different, and what the man had to say was something he had never heard before.

After the magic lantern show was finished the speaker talked to the boys and girls.

He read from the Bible in John 6 v 37 and talked about the bit, "Him that cometh to me I will in no wise cast out."

Some of the children stayed behind at the end of the meeting to have a closer look at this light machine. The magic lantern. George was one of them.

As they stood there in a semi-circle the man spoke to them again.

"Boys and girls, the Lord has promised that him that cometh to Me I will not cast out. If the Lord doesn't cast you out, what must He do with you?" he asked.

There was silence. A deathly hush.

Some of George's friends looked past the speaker at the back wall. Some of them stared down at the floor, pretending to study the knotty pattern in the well-worn wood.

But nobody answered.

The patient gentleman decided to ask his question again. Surely some of them must know the answer.

"If the Lord doesn't cast you out, what must He do with you?" he repeated.

George was embarrassed. The answer was so simple. Yet his friends, the people who came here every week, wouldn't answer the man. They just stood around becoming redder and redder, scratching their heads, shuffling their feet, and looking anywhere but at him.

George raised his hand. Slowly, tentatively. He was just a guest. The new boy.

The speaker spotted George's hand. He was glad that somebody appeared to be responding at last.

"Yes" he said, pointing over to George, "what do you think?"

All eyes were focused on him now. "If he doesn't cast you out then He must take you in," George replied.

The man took a step towards George. He saw the eager, intelligent look on the young boy's face.

"That's right son," he said. "You seem to know what you're talking about."

George flushed mildly. It was a simple question and he had answered it. That was all. Nothing world shattering about that.

The preacher was drawn to this bright boy. He felt he should continue the contact.

"Are you saved son?" he inquired.

George didn't answer.

"Would you not like to be saved?" was the next question.

Unusually, George was lost for words.

He had relieved an awkward situation. Fair enough.

He had answered the man's question. Fair enough.

But he hadn't bargained for this.

He didn't know what the speaker meant. He had never heard about "being saved" in his life before. How could he know whether he wanted it or not?

The puzzled look on the child's face prompted the preacher to put it another way. By now everybody was watching George.

What would he do?

What would he say?

"Would you like to go to heaven?" he continued.

This was something George did want to do. He wanted to go to heaven. Sometime. In fact he had never really considered going anywhere else when the time came.

"Yes." George found his voice at last. "Yes, Yes," he stumbled out. "I would like to go to heaven."

The speaker's face lit up. "We would all like to go to heaven, wouldn't we?" he replied, making a general gesture to all the waiting children.

Turning back to direct his attention to George he said, "Well you have just told me how to get to heaven. Come to Jesus and He will not cast you out. He will make you His child, and He will take you to heaven."

It was becoming simpler now. The fog was clearing.

"Would you like to come to Him now?" was the next penetrating question, gently asked.

"I would," said George.

And he did.

Standing there in that little hall, with some friends around him, George simply, innocently, silently, asked God to save him. He asked the Lord Jesus to take him in, and be his Saviour.

And He did.

George was saved.

That was the most memorable event of his childhood days in Belfast. No doubt about it.

As he walked home later and his friends disappeared one by one up alleyways and behind brightly painted doors, George was pleasantly confused.

He was convinced that what he had done was right. God wouldn't cast him out either and that had to be good. He was happy about that.

There were many, many things, however, that George in his boyish mind didn't know or understand.

He didn't know about the joy he had caused in heaven over a child putting simple faith in Christ.

He was sure his parents wouldn't understand it. George's mum and dad were kind, sincere, hard-working, clean-living people. But they weren't Christians. Not yet.

He didn't know either that Satan wouldn't be pleased.

He wasn't, and he was going to show it

George was to find that out.

CHAPTER 2

The Little Twister's Prayer

George and Roy looked forward to Thursday evening every week. Thursday evening was special. It was pocket-money time. The two boys used to sit in the house listening for the sound of their father's lorry stopping outside. As they heard him close the driver's door they sat up as best they could, waiting for him to come in.

He never disappointed them. In he came, and putting his hand into his pocket produced two single shillings. A shilling for George, and a shilling for Roy.

George had a plan for his pocket money every week. He spent sixpence on sweets, and sixpence on going to the pictures. That pattern of expenditure never varied. The only thing that ever changed was his choice of sweets. But he never missed the pictures. He always went with his friends to the Saturday matinee, having discussed with them the merits of the film that was coming many times before they even saw it.

Now George had a problem. He was a Christian and glad of that. He was trying hard to be happy, but becoming increasingly more unpleasantly confused.

People who appeared to know told him of three new commandments that came along with this "Christianity." He obviously hadn't read the small print.

He hadn't heard these commandments before. He didn't learn them in School. He learnt the Ten Commandments in his R.E. classes.

"Thou shalt have no other gods before me."

"Thou shalt not make unto thee any graven image" and so on. He knew those ones.

The three new ones were different. They read like this.

The first commandment is, "Thou shalt not speak to, associate with, or generally make a friend of anyone who is not a believer."

The second is like unto it. "Thou shalt not run round with most of your old friends any more for 'they say bad words'."

And the third commandment is, "Thou shalt not ever go to the Saturday matinee in the picture-house."

George realised that he was expected to have some sort of sense of moral intuition that made him capable of learning, knowing, inwardly digesting and duly acting upon these commandments from the very moment that he became a Christian.

He felt as though he was being choked, strangled and smothered all at once.

Little boy saved, but with no one to tell him about, or lead him into the joys of the Christian life. About the things that Christians actually DO.

It appeared to him that he was to become an isolated vegetable. Like a worm-eaten, half-hollow, squashy-ended potato left lying alone on the top of the soil at the end of the season. With all its mates stored away in a sheltered barn somewhere.

He thought he must be the most miserable child in East Belfast.

His newly found faith, instead of being a source of comfort and happiness to him was gradually becoming like a great burden on his back.

Nobody asked him to go back to "the wee meetin'."

He had nobody to tell him about Bible reading and prayer.

He couldn't enjoy the companionship of other Christians. He didn't know any.

The most mentally-morally-mixed-up time of all came on a Saturday afternoon.

The matinee.

George watched his friends as they set off chattering to

the picture-house. They were full of eager anticipation of the film they were going to see.

On wet Saturdays he sat in the house. Idly blowing his breath on the window as he watched the droplets of rain running down in crooked paths. He wondered if they were happy.

On dry Saturdays he wandered around the streets near his house. Lazily kicking a stone, or a tin, or a stick here and there. Just to pass the time until a quarter-to-five when his friends would return.

When they came back it wasn't much better either.

Not only did they talk about the film now. They were starting to act it out.

If it had been a Robin Hood film it was all pretend bows-and-arrows.

If it had been a cowboys-and-Indians film you had pretend guns as well as your pretend bows-and-arrows.

And all accompanied by the appropriate sound effects.

George had nothing. He felt left out. Empty.

The natural leader had now become a reluctant spectator. He didn't understand why he couldn't go to the matinee. He didn't even have a holier-than-thou, oh-what-a-good-boy-am-I feeling.

He was just plain miserable.

Then one day George remembered something. It came to him in a flash.

He remembered somebody saying, or teaching him - or perhaps he had read it somewhere. If you asked God for anything in Jesus' name then He would do it. He promised. And God cannot lie.

That was it!

That was the answer!

Late one afternoon George climbed the stairs into his bedroom in the little two-bedroomed spick-and-span street house in which he lived.

There wasn't a lot of space to spare in that bedroom. There was a double bed for George and Roy, a dressing table and a wardrobe. A big old walnut wardrobe.

George got down on his knees beside his bed. He was jammed between the double bed and the wardrobe. He was preparing to pray.

He had chosen a time when there was nobody else in the house so that he could speak out and talk to God quite freely.

And he did.

Taking a firm hold of the bedcover with both hands, and closing his eyes tightly, George prayed.

"Lord, I can't stick this Christianity, but I don't want to go to hell. They tell me if I ask anything in Jesus' name You will do it.

So I ask you now in Jesus' name, save me again two years before I die.

Amen."

When he had finished that prayer happiness began trickling back. George was convinced in his boyish mind that he had put God in a corner from which He couldn't escape. He was tied up to His own promise, on His own terms.

Relaxing his grip on the bedcover he smoothed it down carefully so that nobody would notice a crumpled-up bit.

He rose from his bedside and straightened himself.

He turned his back upon God.

And left the room.

Now he could live, as he liked.

Or so he thought!

CHAPTER 3
The Little Door

Growing up on the streets of East Belfast in the mid-fifties was tough for the teenager. It was gang warfare, razor slashings or bicycle chain fights on many nights of the week. For safety the teenage males roamed in packs. It was dangerous to be caught out alone.

Top-of-the-fashion trendy gear for the young-man-of-the-fifties, teddy-boy type, was shoulder-padded finger-tip length jacket, with sleeves especially designed to hide fingers adorned with knuckle-duster rings, and really tight drainpipe trousers. The tighter they were, the tougher you were. Matching, but essential accessories for this outfit were crepe-soled shoes, string tie, carefully concealed bicycle chain and studded belt. No self-respecting "TED" would ever forget his comb either, to keep his "Tony Curtis" D.A. haircut in order.

When not engaged in a bicycle-chain fight, or preparing for one, or recovering from one, the chief occupation of these endlessly idle teenagers was standing around. In groups or gangs at the street corners.

"Watching all the girls go by."

And commenting on "the talent."

Very pleasant on clear-skied, short-skirted summer evenings. Lovely. But the dull, dark often damp and duffle-coated winter evenings were different. It was hard to pass the time. The time dragged, the girls weren't going by, and if you didn't end up soaking wet you were at the very least freezing cold.

It was on just such an evening that George and a mate were standing at their usual corner. They had their jacket collars up as protection from the biting wind, even though they thought that they were on the sheltered side of the comer. They blew into their cupped hands and stamped their feet to keep warm. They thought it was going to rain. There was very little chat. It was quiet and cold and dull. An endurance test.

Suddenly, almost startling in its suddenness came an invitation from George's mate. It was as though it was something that he had to do to get over with. Like swallowing unpleasant medicine.

He turned to George and said abruptly, "Hey Geordie, me da told me to ask you if you'd go to a Christian meeting?"

A look of bewilderment crossed George's face.

"A Christian meeting," he retorted. "What's that?"

It was the turn of the friend to be astonished now.

"You're kiddin' George," he exclaimed. "Surely you must know what a Christian meeting is!"

George didn't know what a Christian meeting was. He had never been to one. He hadn't a clue.

"Is it like a church?" he asked. "With pillars and wee coloured windows and a man in a black robe chanting and making echoes all round the place. Is that a Christian meeting?"

His mate was mildly amused. "No, George. No. No. It's nothing like that," he replied. "But forget it. I asked you to go and we don't want to go anyway. So just forget it."

George thought for a moment, gave a few giant thumps of his crepe-soled shoes on the pavement to restore the circulation to his feet and then spoke. He had an idea. A very practical one.

"Hold on a minute there," he began, "would there be any HEAT in a Christian meeting?"

"Oh yes, there certainly would. There would be heat there. It would probably be lovely and warm." was the reply.

"Well, come on then. We'll go. We are going to be foundered to death standing here, and we will probably get soaked as well before the night's out. Come on. We're going."

So off they went the pair of them.

To a Christian meeting.

As they walked down the long corridor leading into the Wellington Hall they felt a bit odd. Everybody hustling along beside them seemed sure of themselves. And glad to be going to "a Christian meeting."

The warmth of the music drew them, however. The piano and organ were being played. Lively, inviting music.

They decided to go up to the gallery. They would see more from there. And it would probably be warmer.

It took them a few minutes to find two seats together. They did eventually. The hall was packed. A capacity crowd.

George loved singing. But he had never heard music like this before. These people sang chorus after chorus. Enthusiastically. They really seemed to enjoy it!

One piece touched the two teenage teddy-boys on the gallery. The leader had everybody singing.

"Everybody ought to know,
Everybody ought to know,
Everybody ought to know,
Who Jesus is."

It was the part-singing that got to them. The men sang one part and the women sang another. All in perfect harmony.

It was lovely. It was moving.

And the circulation was coming back to toes and fingers, hands and feet. Their cheeks were beginning to glow. They weren't used to this eye-watering warmth. It was all so cosy.

Later on a man started to speak to the hushed congregation.

It was obvious to the two teenage tearaways that there was something different about this place. God was here. They felt it. They knew it. But they didn't understand it.

One thing they did understand though. They understood that the man was in earnest about whatever it was he was talking about. He talked about the Bible. He pleaded with the people. There was still warmth about it. The warmth of someone sincerely pleading.

Encouraging the people to come to Christ.

At the end of the meeting the speaker made an appeal - and the music played. Softly.

He moved forward to the microphone and leaning forward further still he spoke into it, gently.

"Come down from the balcony
And go through this little door."

He pointed to a little door at the front of the hall beside the platform.

"Come forward from the back of the hall
And go through this little door.
There someone will speak to you,
And tell you what to do."

And he pointed to the little door - again.

The music played softly and the voice soothed the air, above the creak of the chairs and the shuffle of feet.

"Come forward. Don't hold back.
Come to the Lord Jesus.
Come forward now and go through this little door."

George was already pulling himself stiffly to his feet when he looked around at his mate and said, "I'm going to have to go forward. I need to get right with God."

He felt himself being moved by a power beyond his control.

Obviously his friend was having the same experience. He just said, "Me too. I'm going forward as well."

So off they went the pair of them.

To be counselled in a Christian meeting.

As they moved down those aisles towards that little door they weren't alone. There were others, many others, with them. Some with heads bowed. Some weeping silently. All sincerely seeking.

Seeking Jesus. Seeking peace.

The music - the soft inviting strains of "Just as I am without one plea" pervaded the place.

To George and his friend it was almost unreal. Body, soul and spirit felt detached. They couldn't explain how they felt, but they knew they wanted to get right with God.

The atmosphere was charged. Charged with the power and presence of God.

It was spiritually sensitive. Divinely delightful. Great.

At last they came to the little door.

And went through it.

It was like having a child's bucket of seawater thrown round you when you were sunbathing -sleeping on a hot-sand beach on a sunny day.

It was a shock to the system.

When the door, the little door, closed behind them, and the strains of the music ceased, everything turned cold.

The meeting itself had been warm and inviting. Now George and his mate felt they were back to the cold and grey. Quiet and dull. Almost like being back at the corner -only not just quite so cold.

The little door opened into a long room. Chairs and benches sat higgledy-piggledy around the perimeter. Some were there by arrangement. Others were there by just chance. Sitting anywhere.

On some of the chairs there were people. In groups and pairs. In each group or pair there seemed to be somebody with a book. They were usually the ones bent forward.

Some people were still weeping. One or two were kneeling at their chairs. The walls were part-panelled part-painted. That is, where the paint hadn't been peeled off. In a sticky-tape-shaped strip.

In the middle of this room there now stood George and friend. Looking grossly out-of-place. Total misfits, in their padded jackets, crepe-soled shoes, narrow ties and Tony Curtis haircuts.

A kindly man - a boss-man, an organiser, came over to speak to them.

"Can I help you fellas?" he asked with genuine concern.

George looked at him intently and replied, "Well, it's just like this, sir. The man out there told us that if we came through that little door someone in here would tell us what we have to do."

The man was nonplussed. "I'm sorry, boys," he began, "I didn't realise you were seeking God. I thought you were just down here a message. That's why I left you standing to the end. I apologise. I really do."

He was in a dilemma. Here were two young men seeking God, having had the courage to come down and stand patiently in their ridiculous outfits and wait for him. He was determined to do something about it. And fast.

After glancing around for help, which didn't appear to be forthcoming, he turned to George and his mate and said, "All the counsellors seem to be busy at the minute. We will have somebody free to speak to you soon."

Just as he was about to walk away he spotted a young minister as far away from the action as he could possibly be. Hiding almost, it appeared, up the corridor. He had himself flattened against the wall. Wondering which way to run.

"Your reverence," he called over to him, not so loud as to disturb the other groups. "Would you like to counsel these two young men?"

The minister came over to the two by now quite uncomfortable teenagers. He had a pleasant smile. But it was obvious to the two friends that he felt uneasy. Perhaps it was their incongruous appearance, but they didn't think so. It was deeper than that.

"Nice to see you boys," he said. (The stock whatever-are-we-going-to-do-with-these-boys welcome.) He looked around furtively. Like a rat looking out of a drainpipe, seeking a means of escape.

"We will go down to the back of the hall," he said, "where we can find a space for ourselves." With that he strode out, a few paces ahead of his new charges, past the other groups intently talking, to the back of the chilly room. There certainly was no heat in there.

As the three of them stood in a group the young minister looked at George and his friend and asked "What exactly is it that you boys want? What do you want me to do?"

The teddy boys were taken aback. Flabbergasted.

George, always the spokesman, looked at him with amazement and said, for a second time, "The man on the platform in there told us that if we came through that little door someone would tell us what we should do."

"I know," he said. The young man was embarrassed. "But I have only been in this job for a few months and everybody expects me to know everything about the Bible. I tell you what. If I pray with you and ask God to give you whatever it is that you need - would that do you?"

"Oh yes, yes certainly," the two boys replied, almost in unison. "That would be great. Dead on."

By now anything at all would have been great. If only they could get out of that counselling room.

So the minister prayed with them. Placing a hand on each of their heads he asked God to bless them and give them whatever it was that they needed.

Just after he had mumbled, "Amen," and before he could ask, "O.K. then chaps?" the two sixteen-year-olds were on their feet.

"O.K. sir. O.K. and thanks," they said, back over their shoulders as they made for the door, clearly marked EXIT, at the other end of the room.

It led on to a corridor. The corridor led out to the street.

Stopping only long enough to light up a butt, the two boys started for home. As hard as they could go.

It had rained when they were in the Christian meeting. There were puddles on the pavements now. The two escapees were running so hard that their crepe-soled feet splashed water half-way up the shop fronts, leaving it to run back down in dirty indecisive trickles. The smoke from the cigarettes, which they didn't have the time or the breath to smoke, traced funny patterns in the air as they ran.

As they ran they were each convinced -totally convinced, of one thing. Christianity was a hoax. A take-on. The biggest con trick known to man.

And as for Christians. They were all moon men. Space cadets. Freaks and fanatics.

George wanted nothing to do with Christians and Christianity. From henceforth and forever.

He was just going to continue running. Running away. Away from God. His running was to lead him down many dark alleys and one-way streets.

CHAPTER 4
You Pick What You Plant

George continued on his carefree way, running and running and running away. Running away from God.

These running-away years were filled with drinking and petty crime. Generally getting up to no good. And he felt he always got away with it. Some of his mates were caught. Others had very narrow escapes. But George never did. It was great.

There was one little thing that worried him occasionally. Just a bit, and now and again. Like a stone in your shoe on a long walk. Niggling away.

It was a verse. Something that he had heard somewhere. Or did he hear somebody read it from the Bible? Perhaps it was an echo from the Crusade?

"Whatever a man sows, that shall he also reap."

You pick what you plant. You drink what you brew.

Yet it all seemed irrelevant. He tried to forget about it. Anyhow it didn't apply to him. Did it? He was getting off with it.

George loved crowds. He loved to work with people. Crowds of people.

Picking their pockets.

The Ideal Home Exhibition and the Balmoral Show were perfect hunting grounds. Happy out-for-the-day people. Full pockets and bulging wallets. Sunny days and crushing crowds. Narrow alleyways for lightning getaways. Unattended baskets and purses. Packets of cigarettes peeping out of hip pockets. Easy prey for a perceptive pickpocket.

Where was God?

It would be hard to go though those runaway days and

light fingered ways without an occasional fright. To keep the adrenalin flowing. Nothing serious though.

Nothing that a couple of some-sleep-lost nights wouldn't cure.

George loved to plan a shoplifting spree. Standing at the corner with his mates they would discuss the best shops to go to, the best time of the day to go, and the easiest escape route. Or lying in bed at night. Just at that drowsy-dropping-over time he would be thinking of all those shops, and all those shelves and all that stuff....

And George loved Christmas. People and parcels and presents. Families and friendship and fun.

Put the two together and it was a super-thrill for a thinking thief.

George planned carefully for one Christmas. He knew what he wanted for his father and mother. He knew what he wanted for his brother and sister.

So he went out and bought the boxes!

A flat rectangular box for the nylons for mother.

A small box for a diary for Roy.

A long thin box for a pen for father.

No problem with Moira's jewellery. Some colourful Christmas wrapping paper would do for it!

Then he went out and pinched the lot. He had been eyeing them out from Halloween. He knew exactly where they all were. In easily accessible positions in ill-attended shops.

He brought them home, one by one, and matched them up with the waiting presentation boxes. One night when he had all his "presents" in the house and everybody else out of it, he wrapped them up as-best-he-could in fancy Christmas paper. "Borrowed" as well. Then he returned them all to their separate and secret hiding places, and waited for Christmas.

Christmas Eve arrived at last. George and family shared the joy and warmth of the season around the cheery fire in the tiny kitchen house. The smell of Christmas cooking filled the air. Neighbours came and went. Everybody wished everybody "A Happy Christmas." Presents were exchanged. Appreciation was shown in various ways. Through a word and a smile to a hug or a kiss.

Just one person was missing that evening. Pity, but father had to work late. It was always busy around Christmas time in the fruit business.'

George and Roy went to bed before father came home. But not to sleep. Just to lie and chat and laugh and listen for the lorry. They wanted to hear father's reaction to his presents. He might even come up to say "Thanks" and it wouldn't do to be sleeping.

At last the lorry came. Rumbling up the street. They knew the sound of it. They had heard it so many times before. And only one lorry door on the Avoniel Road made a tin-boom echo like their father's when given a hearty thank-goodness-I'm-home-at-last bang.

They heard the front door opening and in came father.

It was late. He was tired. But he had presents too. Some fruit from the market - some exotic hard-to-get-things "wee treats for Christmas," he called them, and some half-rotten have-to-be-used-up before-the-holidays-are-over stuff. He had a bag of other presents as well. A few wrapped like-a-man-does boxes.

The atmosphere in the bedroom was expectant. What would he think of his presents? What would he say? Would he like them? Would he be up?

They lay with bated breath. There was a silence first broken only by the rustle of the ripping of Christmas wrappings. Then an unexpected reaction.

Was that signs of anger? Was Daddy rearin' up? When George's da reared up, he sat up. But this time he jumped up - and ran to the top of the stairs.

Taking hold of the cream-painted banister rail he leaned over to hear more. What was this all about?

Then it came. The voice was raised. "To think that the child saved up his pocket-money to buy me a pen like that and the thing doesn't even work! Just wait till after Christmas!

I'm going down to that shop and I'll give them boys a piece of my mind!"

George DIDN'T have a very happy Christmas that year. The turkey tasted like sawdust and the ginger-wine was as tame as lemonade. Was he going to be caught on? Was he going to reap the harvest now? After Christmas? Surely not?

It was close-really close. It was wrong. George knew he had done the right thing in the wrong way. But it hadn't caught up with him just yet.

By the time Christmas was over and the shops were open again George's daddy had forgotten his anger. And George knew his daddy and presents. He liked to receive them but he hardly ever used them. On Boxing Day daddy put all his presents away in the drawer where he had been stacking them up for years. That evening, during a lull in the festivities, George paid a visit to the drawer and hid the pen amongst the seventeen pairs of never-to-be-worn socks that lived at the back. Just in case. Then he breathed more easily again.

For a while at least.

As he became more involved in petty crime George almost forgot about the verse. Almost. But not quite. It had an annoying habit of raising its aggravating head in two recurring sets of circumstances in this unstable environment. One was on near misses such as the Christmas pen and the other was on visits to Fir Tree Lodge.

George's grandparents lived in the country. A pleasant place with tall firs, a well-tended lawn and vegetable garden. As a child George had loved the swing amongst the firs. It was a gentle joy on a summer day to sit on the shiny stick pushed through the uncomfortable knot, holding lightly on to the coarse sweet-smelling rope tucked in at his neck, and swing lazily. To and fro and round and round.

He had enjoyed racing Roy across the lawn and back to the house when Granny called them in for tea. Soda-farls fresh off the griddle, dripping with country butter. What a taste!

Now that he was older, the vegetable garden preached to him. He didn't like it.

Whoever it was that had explained that verse had said, "If you sow lettuce, you will grow lettuce. You won't grow scallions. If you sow cabbage, you grow cabbage. You don't grow beetroot."

As George walked along the path beside the weed-free rows, there they all were. Nodding and rustling in the breeze. Lettuce and scallions, cabbage and beetroot. Looking up at him.

"You grow what you sow, George," they said.

"You pick what you plant, George," they said.

A lesson from Nature. A voice from God.

Monday nights were bad nights now. The weekend money was spent. The cigarette packets were empty and had been thrown down somewhere. Discarded. Useless. And where was the drink money going to come from for the rest of the week?

George had learnt from his message-bicycle days that a certain door on a certain street would be opened at five o'clock every day.

Old Marky Moore and his sister kept lodgers, but they had a problem. They were both going deaf and couldn't hear the doorbell. So at five o'clock every weekday work-a-day evening, winter and summer, they left the door off the latch to allow the homecoming boarders access to the house.

George knew this for he used to, when younger, prop the cumbersome, heavy, hard-to-ride and harder-to-steer message bicycle against the wall of the house and push the front door with a box of groceries. And low and behold -it opened!

Useful piece of information for an unscrupulous stony-broke teddy boy on a Monday night.

After all, there must have been fifteen coats hanging in that hall. Just hanging on hooks on a board on the wall in the hall. Two and sometimes three on top of each other. Waiting to be rifled. Easy pickings.

Every Monday evening then, after the door was opened - and before the lodgers came home, George was up the hall and had his drink money for the week. He was very particular. He didn't disturb anything and he didn't destroy anything. He never took more than a few pounds either, and always from a different coat. That way nobody would ever miss it. Then he could come back next week.

Next Monday was going to be smokeless and dry also!

CHAPTER 5

Did God Say?

During the years that followed the teddy-boy era George read the Bible.

Surprise, surprise!!

Perhaps not so surprising.

George didn't read the Bible because he loved it.

George didn't read the Bible out of any deep desire to study it.

He just dipped in and out of it. Like a child going for its first bathe in the sea too early in the year. Want to be in it but it is really too deep and too frightening and too cold yet.

He read the Bible for two reasons. Two entirely different reasons. One was that he occasionally read it seeking some sort of comfort or solace. Especially in those moments of dire extremity when he would be heart-broken as a consequence of his wayward style of life.

One evening he sat in his little bedroom and looked at himself in the dressing table mirror. It was one of those adjustable-at-the-bottom-by-six-inches-only mirrors that always creaked when you moved it. Through the blur of tears he could see his swollen lips, his reddened eyes and bloated face. What he couldn't see was what he could feel. It was breaking his heart. He was miserable. Everything was going wrong. It hadn't been a good night on the town.

"Where is that Bible?" he thought.

He looked in all the possible places. Eventually he found it hiding away in a dressing-table drawer. Placing it almost reverently on the eiderdown he fell to his knees beside the bed.

Again. The twister - a bigger one now - was back. All twisted-up himself. He had opened the book but he didn't know where to read. He had no map of the book. He had no real idea about it. He did read it though. Flicking through it. Reading at random. And everywhere he read it was doom. Doom and gloom.

"Woe unto you," it said.

"Woe is me for I am undone," it said.

"Your iniquities have separated between you and your God," it said.

It all struck terror into the very soul that craved for consolation.

"How does anybody get any comfort from reading that stuff," he thought.

Raising himself on his elbow he flung the Bible across the room and then buried his face in the eiderdown in deep despair. The flying Bible hit the dressing table and fluttered to the floor in a flurry of pages like a wild duck wounded by a spray of gunshot.

He was unable to find the solace he sought in the Scriptures but the wayward style of life continued.

Those female-chasing years and a broken engagement cultivated an even deeper desire for the opium effect of drunkenness.

His disillusionment and cynicism turned him into a scoffer. He mocked anybody who said they were a Christian and pitied the naivety of anybody who said they believed the Bible. How could anyone be so stupid? How could any thinking person be so simple? He wanted to save them from themselves. Waken them up. Open their eyes.

So he read the Bible. He needed a case. He needed ammunition to hit them with when he got the chance. Bring them back to their senses.

This accounted for the uncharacteristic sight of George sitting by the fireside on a winter evening, with a drink in one hand, a cigarette in his mouth, and an open Bible in the other hand.

His well worn but certainly not original challenges of "Where did Cain get his wife?" or "The Bible contradicts itself," or "Who were the sons of God in Genesis chapter six when God has only one Son?" were one line of attack. But they were old chestnuts. Battered and bandied and bashed about for too long. They were beginning to crack and show signs of age. He needed to have something fresher and deeper and different in reserve. George was the cynic of cynics. The prime scoffer. So he had to do his homework.

The main targets for his ammunition, the bulls eye for his Bible busters, were young converts. Those who were fired with the enthusiasm of a fresh new faith.

These were just the people who came to George to witness to him. They wanted to tell him about their "Joy in the Lord" as they called it. What they didn't know was that they were unwittingly incurring his disdain by telling him that they were "praying for" him.

He, in turn, being made aware of their misplaced concern for his spiritual well being, felt obliged to expose the futility of their belief.

He was merciless in his attacks. It was only by being extremely cruel that he could be effectively kind. They had to be warned, these bubbly Christians. They were making fools of themselves he thought.

Through all of those Bible-blasting, convert-crushing days he never encountered anyone who had enough Bible knowledge to stand up to him. To answer his questions. To take him down a peg or two. So it was then, that the young Christians who were asked the questions hadn't had time to learn the answers, and the experts who had all the answers were never asked the questions!

Something else, something big, something important was to happen in those days.

It all began with bikes.

George worked in a supermarket on the outskirts of Belfast, and travelled to work each day on his racing bicycle.

He was proud of his bike and particular about where he

left it. It was a special bike and a special bike needed a special park.

George had one. There was a waist-high wall outside the supermarket, and there was a position on that wall where George left his bike. Every day. Everybody who lived or worked within two hundred yards of the supermarket knew that and respected it. You didn't park your bike, or your pram or even yourself there. That was George's place.

Well, almost everybody knew it.

One autumn morning George rode up to the wall as usual. As he stooped down to remove his bicycle clips he was aware that something was funny. There was nowhere for his bike. Someone had the cheek to leave their bicycle on his spot.

And it was a girl's bike at that!

The sheer humiliation of it!

He would fix her, whoever she was! In a sullen, almost childish rage, he jammed his bike on top of hers entangling the handlebars in such a way as to lock the both of them together. As he stumped across towards the supermarket entrance he spared himself the time for a hasty backward glance over his shoulder. Entering the door of the shop he muttered to himself, "You'll have trouble getting out of that m' girl, whoever you are!"

At the end of that ordinary tea-and-sugar, bread-and-butter day George emerged from his work to find a bewildered office girl from the butcher's shop next door puzzling as to how she was gong to extricate her bike from this mess. She was on the verge of tears. She wanted her bike and she wanted home. That was all.

George felt sorry for her. Something stirred inside him.

"Nice wee thing," George thought to himself as he approached her. "Attractive. Cute wee article. Do all right." He spoke to her, with a charming smile. No sullen rage now.

"Is that your bike?" he asked gently, pointing over to where her bike was trapped, jammed in against the wall.

"Yes it is!" she said, almost angrily, "Is this one yours?"

George walked over with a spring in his step and willingly removed his bicycle from the top of hers. It took him a few minutes. He had made a good job of it. When his bicycle was safely out of the way, leaning against his waist, the young woman moved over to retrieve hers.

It was then that George noticed the tricycle. There had been a little child's tricycle sitting, front-wheel-turned-in, where a child had abandoned it beside the two bikes.

"The tricycle wouldn't be yours as well?" he quipped.

"No it's not," she replied. She was laughing now. As she laughed George noticed a sparkle in that blue eye. The kind of sparkle that says, "She likes me you know."

Could the tricycle have been a sign? A harbinger of things to come?

George and Liz were married on Saturday 14th July, 1962 in Westburn Presbyterian Church on the Newtownards Road in East Belfast!

CHAPTER 6
'I'll Make The Bullets...'

Shortly before the wedding George had taken over a small business on the Lisburn Road in Belfast. Groceries, fruit and vegetables, confectionery and cigarettes. He built it up from almost nothing to a good going concern. He really worked at it!

To be convenient to the shop George bought a house in a nearby street. He wanted something small and compact but somewhere in which he and Liz could enjoy one another's company. Start out in life together. That was the original idea.

Five minutes walk from your wife to your work.

Five minutes walk from your work to your wife.

Sounded ideal for a young married couple. But it didn't work out that way. Far from it.

Liz spent many a lonely vigil in that house. George was hardly ever in.

He was working eighty hours every week. Fifty two weeks in every year. With only four days holiday. Easter Monday and Tuesday, Christmas Day and Boxing Day. That was all. He even spent the Twelfth of July behind a stall on the Lisburn Road. Selling fruit and confectionery, cigarettes and minerals, to the passing crowds'.

Young man though George was -shrewd business operator though George was, he couldn't stick that kind of pressure.

Eventually he had to change. Giving up the business, he moved house to the east end of Belfast where he had been brought up, and took a nine-to-five job in a bacon factory.

He was now free in the evenings to frequent his former

haunts with his old mates. Round the pubs that he knew so well.

He went where he liked and with whoever he liked most nights of the week -but Saturday night was different. It was special. Saturday nights were reserved for drinking with his father-in-law.

George liked his father-in-law. "Da" he called him. He was indeed old enough to be George's "Da" but it didn't seem to make any difference. They got on well together. Great buddies.

They often drank in the Hillfoot Bar. They used to sit there on Saturday evenings surrounded by the chink of the glasses, the stale cigarette smoke filling the air and the constant babble of voices. Recounting stories, telling jokes.

It was a popular whiling-away-the-time occupation, telling jokes. But it was always difficult to remember your joke for a whole evening because the more jokes you heard and the more liquor you consumed, the more befuddled you became. So it was important to get your joke in early on in the proceedings. Nobody ever listened to anybody else's joke for they were too busy remembering their own!

If it wasn't a joke -just a tall story, some still sensible member of the audience would respond, almost convincingly sometimes, with, "Well fancy that!" or "Is that a fact?" or "I don't believe you!"

It was on just such an easy-listening-steady-drinking Saturday night that George had a strange experience. Everything was going as usual. The crowds had gathered into the Hillfoot Bar. They were crushed around the tables in the lounge. Saturday nights were the busiest nights. The glasses were being filled and the booze knocked back with monotonous regularity. The air was becoming thicker with smoke that smarted the eyes. The jokes and stories were succeeding one another thick and fast and being as-politely-as-possible ignored.

George's beady eyes were roving round the bar. Always

on the lookout for who or what he could see. As he looked he talked. He was going through the stock responses.

"Well here that's a good 'un," and "Get away on wi' ye" and "Man I would never have believed it!" slurred through lips holding loosely on to a cigarette.

Slowly he became aware of something. Through the dim haze of partial inebriation a sixth sense kindled in him. It was neither a roaring revelation nor a still small voice. It was just this thought that came creeping into his consciousness.

"You'd better watch out," it warned "or you're going to loose your drinking partner on a Saturday night."

"What's this?" he thought to himself. He was mildly stupefied but returned to reality with a start. He had been miles away -soothed by the sound of the storyteller's voice -and the storyteller was his old friend "Da". He had just been about to interject with another "Is that right? You're kiddin'!" but suddenly he changed his approach. Removing the cigarette from his mouth with two well-stained fingers he blew a thin jet of smoke down amongst the collection of half-empty glasses on the table.

Turning sideways towards his father-in-law he asked, almost sharply, "What was that you were saying there, Da?"

Father-in-law liked George too, but sometime he became a bit exasperated with him. This was one of those times. He rebuked his inattentive son-in-law. Gently but firmly. There was a real rapport between them.

"Am I talking to myself here or what?" he remonstrated. "I have been talking away here George, and you haven't heard a word I've been saying. Not one single word".

It was true, but George didn't have to admit it for Da was continuing, "I was just talking about this fella in the shipyard. A Christian fella. Very decent chap he is and he seems to know what he's talking about."

George could hardly believe his ears. "A Christian?" he said softly. Totally dumbfounded. As the truth of what his father-in-law had been saying began to sink in, George started to shout so that everybody at the table sat up to take notice.

"A Christian! A Christian!" He exclaimed. "Don't be telling me Da that you're over sixty years of age and you haven't found out yet that Christianity is the biggest hoax on God's earth! It's all a lot of baloney! Hogwash!"

"You might say that George, in fact you're always saying that. I've heard you at it many a time before," father-in-law replied evenly, and went on, "but if you heard this fella you would change your tune."

This made George uneasy. Uneasy to the point of becoming rattled.

"I could soon change his tune!" was the angry retort. By now the babble of voices at the nearby tables had become subdued and the glasses clinked less frequently. Everybody within earshot was listening.

"If I had him here I would give him a red face I can tell you. The whole thing's a hoax and I can prove it. I have five questions and I haven't met the Christian yet that has been able to answer even one of them!"

George was regaining his composure as he talked. He was back to an almost-normal voice when he began, "I tell you what I'll do, Da. I'll make the bullets and you take them down to the shipyard and fire them!"

Da smiled wryly. "You don't want me to shoot the man do you George?" he replied. The by now captive audience gave soft sympathetic laughs and the heat had gone out of the situation.

"No, Da, no," George said when the laughter had subsided. "I'll provide you with the questions is what I mean. You take them down to the shipyard and the next time you see this Christian fella you ask them to him. O.K.?"

"O.K. I suppose so." Father-in-law wasn't so sure that it would work but he agreed. Reluctantly.

After one of their many pilgrimages to the toilet Da was duly supplied with the questions. The bullets. It wasn't new ammunition. Just the same old stuff George armed him with.

The marital status of Cain?

The apparent, but in George's words, glaring, contradictions in the Bible.

The sons of God in Genesis six...

Deadly bullets for shooting down Christians!

Soon the conversation changed. Somebody told a joke. Nobody heard but everybody laughed. And so the night wore on.

When George eventually arrived home, very much later, he felt satisfied. Another Christian on the spot. A good night's work. He hoped Da could remember the questions. He was well equipped. If his aim was good his ammunition was lethal.

In his more lucid moments in the next week George's thoughts turned to Da and the shipyard showdown. How was he getting on? Had he asked the questions yet? Had the Christian fella, whoever he was, wised up?

It seemed a long time until the next Saturday night. George could hardly wait. He amused himself by anticipating Da's description of the scene.

"You were right George, you blasted him!" he would say.

"You have really proved it to me once-and-for-all. There is definitely nothing in this Christianity!" he would say.

It would be good. Great, in fact.

Saturday evening came at last. At long last. The same old scene. The Hillfoot Bar. The drinks, the stories, the jokes. George sat beside his father-in-law waiting to be told all about the fella in the shipyard.

Da was very quiet. There were no jokes from him. No laughs. No stories. No Christian. No shipyard. There was something strange going on. George was disappointed. He became aware that his father-in-law was avoiding the subject. Deliberately.

George could stick it no longer. He had been waiting for a week for this moment.

With a nonchalant shrug of the shoulder he turned to him and said, "Da, tell us this here. What about that Christian in the shipyard?"

George's best mate, his drinking partner, looked at him straight in the eye and replied, with obvious reticence, "George, I was hoping you wouldn't ask me that. I know you're not going to like what I have to tell you."

"What do you mean?" George was taken aback. Again.

"What do I mean? I'll tell you what I mean! The man answered every one of your questions. Easy as pie. Just like as if they were Sunday school stuff. Five hard questions! They weren't questions George. They were wee buns! He just ate them up. No problem. Brushed every one of them to the side he did."

All that couldn't be left unchallenged. George's reputation was at stake here. He needed time to think. Nodding to the barman as he passed he called, "Bring us two more pints of Double X and two rum-and-cokes please."

When these were brought to the table George went on the offensive again.

"Da, he's pulling the wool over your eyes because you don't know the Bible. He's bluffing you!"

It was father-in-law's turn to be rattled. He rebuked George severely. In earnest. He really meant it this time.

"Now listen, George," he said. "I want to hear no more of this rubbish. You might think you know more about the Bible than I but I am dead sure of this one thing. I know inside me that what that man in the shipyard is telling me is true. I believe him."

George was finished.

Felled.

Floored.

Flattened.

He said no more.

CHAPTER 7
Please God May I Die?

The long hours and incessant working in the little shop on the Lisburn Road had launched George into a state of mental fatigue and depressing emptiness. He had never known anything like this before.

Why was he suddenly checking everything ten times over?

Where had all his self-confidence gone?

He became aware that he was now in bondage to a power within him that dominated and controlled his entire being. His mind was like a lightless dungeon. The blackness could only be experienced from the inside.

The oppression continued for twenty-four hours out of every day.

No peace ever.

Nothing but worry, anxiety, guilt, regrets, fears.

He longed for death.

In desperation one miserable night he sought it.

George came home late, under the influence of drink. It had been a bad night. Even worse than usual.

Liz was in bed, asleep, as she nearly always was by the time he came home. As he looked at her he was pricked to the heart. He didn't deserve a girl like this.

Lying in bed, staring up at the ceiling, feeling sick and sore, he remembered something.

He remembered prayer. And he thought about God.

"If you ask anything in Jesus name...." they had said. He had used it before. This was something he could try. An emergency exit. He would pray to God in Jesus' name....

He always answered. Didn't He?

So George prayed again. The prayer of a man at the end of his tether. He felt he could take no more of it.

Closing his eyes, more in hope than in reverence, he began, "Dear God, please let me die. I want to die in my sleep. I don't want to wake up. Please God, grant this to me. I ask it in Jesus' name. Amen."

His mind was in torment and his life was in ruins. He had no desire to continue with this misery.

But the prayer should do it. God would answer his prayer and he would die in the night.

People would say - he could imagine it,

"Wasn't it sad about George Bates? Shocking. Very sudden. Must have been a heart attack or something."

He wouldn't care what they said. He would be away. Free. Out of it all.

George kept his eyes closed. He didn't want to open them, for he was just going to sleep away. To vanish from this earth for good.

With the warmth of the bed and the comforting thought of eventual relief he gradually drifted off to sleep...

Only to wake up again!

Daylight was just beginning to peep in at the corners of the roller blind when George realised he was still alive.

"You lied to me! You lied to me!" he cried, swinging his arm in fury. He sat bolt upright in the bed. His flailing arm struck the headboard just above Liz's head and there was a tremendous crash.

By some sinister supernatural power he had split the headboard, a heavy-duty built-to-last-a-lifetime solid wooden headboard split clean in two. Lengthways. The top of it fell hack a few inches against the wall and there it remained. Propped up at a gentle tilt.

Cracked and broken and useless.

Just like George.

Liz was awake by now. But she didn't say anything. George struggled out on to the floor and into his clothes. Without saying anything either.

He went out to work and there wasn't a word spoken about the incident. Not a word.

It worried George all day. What would Liz say? What would she think of him now?

She spent every penny she earned buying essentials to keep the house going. If she ever had anything extra she would buy something special. For the both of them.

All he could do was wreck things on her.

What a miserable-low-down-no-good of a husband.

When he arrived home from work Liz had a meal for him. She always had, but he didn't always come home. They ate the meal and the headboard wasn't mentioned. They sat over to the fire and still she wasn't going to say anything.

George wanted to have the matter cleared. He felt bad about it. He had it all planned out what he was going to say. Hesitantly he began, "I'm sorry about the headboard love, I didn't really mean...."

Liz held up her hand as if to stop the traffic. A twinkle had returned to those blue eyes. Rising up from her chair she touched George lightly on the shoulder, "Come up and see," was her reply.

George was puzzled as he followed her upstairs to the bedroom. What did she mean?

A big surprise was in store when he entered the room. The whole place looked different!

During the day Liz had sawn off the remaining part of the headboard and turned the bed around. The offending stumps were now covered by the bedclothes.

Turning to face her mildly bemused husband she announced proudly, "I always wanted one of them divan beds anyway love!"

It was obvious from the warmth of her sense of humour and her forgiving attitude that she still loved him. Although he was a useless character in his own esteem, she loved him.

And that was always something. And it had to be good.

But he was still alive. And that was something else.

He was alive, but he wasn't living.
And that could only be bad.
Days were drudgery. Nights were misery.
Every day, every week. Every night, every week.
Perhaps his change of job would provide the answer. An avenue of escape. Into oblivion. Out of it all.
He was now employed in an east Belfast bacon factory. Boning the sides of bacon. With deft movements of the hand and wrist he could bone an entire side in a matter of minutes.
He was an expert with a boning knife.
A knife-man, he was called.
George toyed with those knives. Sharp as lances and with points like needles.
Could he end it all with a knife?
At weekends he used to sneak his knife out of the factory to sharpen it. Hidden up a sleeve or in a lunch-box.
There was Saturday nights or early Sunday mornings when he sat in the kitchen looking at that knife. Turning it over and over on the table. Spinning it loosely in his hands. Looking at his miserable reflection in its shiny-razor-sharp blade.
He was so depressed. He was a slave to a cruel master. He was disgusted with himself. His language and his jokes were so vile that nobody wanted to listen to him anymore.
A good-for-nothing wretch was how he felt.
But he couldn't end it with a knife.
He pushed the point against his throat till he felt the prick.
And he took it away again.
He pushed it against his ribs. Could he pierce his own heart?
No. He took it away again.
Although he desperately craved for a release, George realised that this was not the escape hatch. A knife-job would be messy he knew - but that wasn't the reason.
It wasn't that which held him back.

It was the fear. The fear of the blackness of the beyond.
He wanted to die.

But he was scared of death. The afterwards bit.

Days were by now pointless, fruitless, cheerless, empty.

George was living in a hell on earth.

The worry became worse.

The guilt grew greater.

The nights were nightmares.

So he considered the river. The Lagan. He had walked by its side, sat on its banks, and crossed its bridges.

Could he drown himself in its deep dark waters?

On one particularly desperate night he decided to give it a try. Anything was worth a try.

The lights along the river twinkled and flashed. Some were reflected on the shimmering surface. A swan cruised aimlessly, silently, close to the bank farther upstream.

George didn't notice much of that. He wasn't in the mood to appreciate the beauty of his tranquil surroundings. Sitting on the parapet of the King's Bridge he wanted to die. He was going to throw himself over and end it all. What was there to live for anyway?

One good push and he would be off the bridge, through the air and into the river.

And that would be it. The end.

He was still in bondage to the unseen power within him working out his evil lusts. His marriage was at breaking point because of the double life he was leading. He was smoking heavily, drinking steadily, drunk mostly, and totally and absolutely miserable.

He wanted out. He must be liberated.

The chains were choking him. He had to break free.

As he sat on the wall of that bridge he looked down into the murky water. Bits and pieces floated past. A branch with a few leaves left on, a bottle that glinted at certain angles in the lights, an old jagged-ended flooring-plank....

George didn't pay any attention to what was on the water.

He was wondering what it would be like to be in the water. He intended to find that out.

He was determined to jump. Soon.

It was after midnight. Silence enveloped the scene. His tortured mind was besieged by very practical considerations.

I wonder is the water cold? He thought.

If I fall from this height will I hit the bottom? He thought. A muddy bottom would be good. Then I would stick in it and drown all that much quicker.

How long will it take me to die? He thought.

Watching the black water gliding past seemed to bring a rush of thoughts to his numbed brain.

Where will they find my body? Will they know who I was? Will anybody care?

What about Liz -what will she think? She might be sorry for a while, but she will get used to it. Being rid of me will be a relief to her anyway.

Looking downstream he saw the embankments on either side. The streetlights stood in orderly rows adding an orange glow to the scene. Like sentries at this river of death. Farther down some now-and-again traffic crossed the Ormeau Bridge.

There was hardly any traffic at all on his bridge at this time of night. That was why he had chosen it.

It was quiet. Almost deserted. He could jump in here and nobody would ever see or know.

The longer he sat there the colder he became. And the colder he became the more difficult it seemed to become to jump. To take his own life.

He wanted to. He really wanted to.

But there was still the fear. The nagging fear. This afterwards thing.

What if it isn't the end?

What if death doesn't finish it all?

Would there be even the remotest chance that the hell he would launch himself into could be worse than the torment of mind he was in?

Would there?

For if there would be then he couldn't do it. He just couldn't jump. Not tonight.

The chill of the night had penetrated his very bones and was bringing him back to his senses. It was almost two a.m.

There was nobody at all about now.

He decided against it.

He would just go home.

George turned round from facing the river to facing the road. It was difficult to swing his legs back over the wall of the bridge for they were so stiff and he was almost numb with cold. Pushing himself off the parapet he landed on the narrow pavement. When he hit the footpath he could hardly stand. His knees were locked and his feet were tingling with "pins and needles".

He clung onto the wall until mobility returned. Then he set off for home.

He hadn't done it. He hadn't jumped.

He had been too scared.

His fear of death had overcome his desire to die. Another time.

As he walked along the embankment towards the Ormeau Road he kept looking at the river.

Why could I not do it? he thought to himself. Why do I always draw back? He consoled himself with the fact that there would always be another night.

"I'll be back. I'll be back. I'll be back" he kept mumbling, as he stumbled homewards.

On reaching his own front door George fumbled for his key and let himself into the house as quietly as he could. Some semblance of sense and sanity were returning now. He climbed the stairs silently, not wanting to awaken his sleeping wife and son. He was a father now. Something, which deepened his sense of worry and guilt.

It was the middle of the night.

As he pushed open the bedroom door, the light from the

landing streamed in to reveal Liz peacefully sleeping and their little son in bed beside her. Where he should have been.

The little one only two years old, had climbed out of his cot in the room next door and had found his way into bed beside his mum. Warmth and comfort for both of them. He was lying at an angle. Almost across the pillow end. His head was touching his mummy's shoulder. A picture of cosy contentment.

George closed the door so that only a shaft of light entered the room. He crossed to the bottom of the bed. Stood staring down at them, asleep.

He was dejected. Totally and utterly.

Looking at his sleeping son he said under his breath, "Wait till you find out son, the kind of louse you have got for a father."

He felt so guilty. He had wanted to die. He STILL wanted to die. But how could he leave them?

George was a man in chains. Firmly fettered by his own folly. It seemed impossible to break free. He didn't know what to do or where to turn.

The sense of guilt was overwhelming. And the fear. There was always the fear. The fear of life. The fear of death. The fear of every thing.

He was tormented by fear.

Tormented by fear and tortured by guilt.

Gripping the board at the foot of the bed George just gazed and gazed. Transfixed.

Hot scalding tears trickled down his cheeks and dropped onto the bedcover at his wife's feet as she slept. Blissfully unaware.

Eventually he slipped into the bed. Into what little space there was left for him. To try and snatch a few hours fitful sleep before the morning.

The morning. The morning!

George hated the thought of the morning. Then the whole horrendous routine would begin all over again.

CHAPTER 8
The Hopeless Helps

During those suicidal restless days George was searching for peace. He was craving for a settled happiness that he hadn't known since childhood. But where was it to be found?

He had spent days and nights on drinking sprees. There had been holiday weekends when George had been permanently drunk. He had tried to drown his sorrows in the drink. They just kept on floating to the top of the foaming glass and exploding in the bubbles. Mocking him.

No peace there. No satisfaction.

He needed to seek outside help. He knew that.

But who?

Or where?

Or how?

Where would he even start?

He decided that a good place to begin would be the doctor's surgery. George had the greatest respect for doctors and nurses. This respect was to increase and deepen with the passing of time.

But what would a doctor know about this?

Sick-at-heartness. Searching-for-peaceness.

He looked so tired. It had been a busy day in the surgery. His eyes had a glazed and distant look in them as George slated his personal dilemma.

When he had finished, as much at least as he felt he could tell, the doctor gave a polite cough and said, "Well now, I'll write you a prescription."

What good was a prescription for a guilt complex?

George thanked the doctor, left the surgery, took the

prescription to the chemist, and determined to seek a second opinion from a fresher doctor.

Probably early in the morning.

The second opinion was as fruitless as the first.

A different doctor, another prescription, a change of chemist - but that was all.

No relief. No peace. No rest.

So where did he go from here?

What about the herbalist? There was one in the city centre. He had passed it many a time. Perhaps he could help. George decided it was worth a try. Anything was worth a try in his ceaseless search for peace.

He phoned to make an appointment.

When the day came George-all-dressed-up went down to the herbalist.

Stepping into the large room the prospective patient was ushered to a comfortable seat before a massive desk.

Behind the desk in an even plusher chair sat the herbalist. He was the full of the chair and looked the part. Well-dressed, in his fifties, greying hair and oozing confidence.

It was all very reassuring. Nobody could work in this grandeur unless he had been very successful for many years, was George's initial impression.

"Don't worry young man." the herbalist said after the tale of frustrated emptiness had been poured out, yet again. "Of course we can help you."

On hearing that George was relieved, but in a certain sense also just a little apprehensive, fearing yet another disappointment.

He tried to hide his misgivings as he replied with obvious relief. "That's wonderful. Will you give me the medicine? I'll pay anything you ask for. I don't care what it costs."

Unable to understand his patient's craving for some magical soothing elixir the herbalist became just a little more cautious. "Well it's not just as simple as all that," he continued, "but we can definitely help you."

"What do you mean?" George asked, puzzled.

"We will have to find the best medicine to suit your particular problem. You will understand that what suits one person mightn't suit another," he explained. "Every patient presents a different need." With that he swivelled round silently in his comfortable chair and pointed to a bottle at the left hand side of the top shelf behind him. It was a dark green colour.

"We'll start with this bottle and work our way across the shelf," he said, smiling. George looked at the bottle and then across at the shelf. There seemed to be dozens of bottles of all shapes and sizes containing liquids of almost every conceivable colour on that one shelf.

And it was only the top shelf. There were four more below it!

George thought, "Now I know how you are kept in these magnificent surroundings."

He could imagine himself joining the ranks of the hundreds who made regular pilgrimages to this herbal paradise with a fiver in their pockets, for another bottle of a different colour!

After duly purchasing his own trial bottle of the recommended remedy George set off for home on the red double-decker bus. Halfway up the Castlereagh Road he uncorked the bottle and drank a couple of mouthfuls. He couldn't wait to get home.

His confidence in his cure was severely dented when he discovered that it was just like tasteless coloured water.

He finished the course within a few days but never went back to the herbalist.

He could be going there till he was ninety, or broke, and still have no peace.

Should he try the chemist?

The next few months were spent in consuming every tonic, powder or dose that could possibly be suited to George's chronic need.

They made absolutely no difference. None at all.

It was all to no avail.

The search for peace was fruitless. His life was empty, his mind was in turmoil. He had no peace. No joy. No satisfaction.

One night, quite by chance, George met some of his old Teddy-boy mates. Grown up now. A bit more settled and with a bit more sense.

As they chatted in the street one of them remarked casually, "Did you hear about that young girl who went to the spiritist woman at the Hollywood Arches?"

"No, no" was the response. "What happened?"

"Well I don't know what the spiritist woman did or said, but a young girl went to her one night and came straight out of her place and threw herself under a bus."

"Funny," said somebody.

"Very odd," said somebody else. Then the conversation changed.

On his way home that night, George was thinking about the spiritist. If she has that sort of power, he reasoned, maybe she could do something for me. It too was worth a try.

Next day he made an appointment and went to see the spiritist. He went seeking help but found none. She had no power to do anything for him. There was no help from the devil for him. After all he was George's master, and wasn't going to let him go. Not that easily.

Months later, many miserable months later, a hypnotist came to Belfast. The papers were full of it; the billboards were plastered with it, "World Famous Hypnotist Comes to Belfast."

Now this is the answer, thought George. He can give me peace. If he could hypnotise me then all my worries and guilt and fear would go. I must see him.

So George went to the Empire Theatre. He went to see the show. Very impressive. People doing daft things at a word from the hypnotist. If he could just say "When I count five and snap my lingers you will have peace of mind" wouldn't it be great?

As the people filed out of the theatre, marvelling at the power of the hypnotist, George sought out an attendant.

Going straight up to him, he made his request, "I would like to make a private appointment to see the hypnotist. I will pay anything he asks. Don't worry about the money bit of it. I must see him as soon as possible."

"I don't know whether he would see you privately or not," was the astonished man's reply, "But did you know that he lives in Belfast? His number will be in the phone book."

George left the Empire Theatre and as he passed the Albert Clock on his way home he said to himself, "I'll be ringing that man first thing tomorrow morning."

It meant waiting another day, but he would wait any length of time for anything, or anybody, who could bring peace or rest or happiness to his broken heart.

Setting the receiver down in the telephone kiosk next morning, after date, time, location and fee had all been arranged, George felt a measure of satisfaction. A glimmer of hope was flashing on and off in the distance of his troubled mind.

At last, here was someone who could help. His confidence was even further boosted when he met the hypnotist. He was every inch a showman in private just the same as in public.

"I can easily help you," he said after hearing George's story and his quest for peace. "Let me first explain something to you."

This was comforting. George was going to have something explained to him. It would be marvellous if he could have everything explained to him. Like why he felt so miserable or why he couldn't sleep or why he had never any peace of mind, ever.

Everything might be a bit too much to ask though. Something would always be a start.

"Ever heard of the commandos?" The hypnotist began with a question.

"Yes, I have," George said, nodding his head but wondering at the same time what the commandos had to do with him.

"They were always first in and last out of battle situations." He wasn't going to have to wait long for an explanation. "And

59

do you know what they did in battle if they had a dreadful injury? An arm or a leg shot off or something like that. If they couldn't bear the pain before the medical teams arrived they were taught how to hypnotise themselves."

"Is that right?" George was interested. Hopeful-at-last.

"Yes, that's right," the hypnotist continued. "Now I'm going to teach you how to hypnotise yourself so that when you have these feelings of guilt and fear and whatever else it is that you have then you can get rid of them yourself. Easily. It will only take you fifteen or twenty minutes in any day."

"That sounds good," said George. "That's just what I want. That's what I've been looking for, for years."

"Let's go then," said the hypnotist. "We're going on a trip to a desert island. To launch yourself on this exciting voyage the sign will be this," and he touched himself lightly on the left cheek with the first and middle finger of his left hand. "Do that George," he instructed.

The by-now willing subject touched himself lightly on the left cheek as directed. It seemed such a small price to pay for such a big relief - peace of mind.

"You are now walking on a beautiful beach on an uninhabited desert island," the hypnotist began softly. "The breakers are coming rolling in, foaming and white and the gulls are wheeling overhead. Can you hear them crying? The palms are waving to you and the sun is warm on your back and the sand is warm under your feet. It is falling away as you tramp on it. You are there alone - you and your spade.

You are walking down towards the sea.

It is breaking over the rocks just out there, sending showers of spray to sparkle in the sunlight.

Begin to dig now. There at the edge of the water. Use your spade. That's right, take it slowly at first. The sand is firm and digs away easily. Good. Notice how every spadeful is making the hole ten times bigger. That's great. Look down into the hole you have dug. Can you see the bottom? No. You can't. There is no bottom to this hole.

Lay your spade down. Just there on the sand beside the

hole. Now think of all those things that worry you. All your anxieties, fears, hang-ups, regrets, guilt-complexes. Your broken heart. Everything that is making you so unhappy. Bind them up in separate parcels. That's good. Now you have a big pile of parcels beside you.

Look down the hole. The sun is so warm your back is beginning to get sunburnt. Feel it tingling? You had better hurry though, for the tide is coming in quickly.

Pick up those parcels one by one and throw them down the hole. Watch them go. There go your fears. See the parcel bouncing off the sides as it goes out of sight. There goes your heartache. There go those anxieties. They have all disappeared too. Hurry, hurry, here comes the tide!

Good! That's them all! Pick up your spade and run!

Sit down there below that coconut palm. The shade will be welcome. You are out of breath. Now watch. The tide is coming in. It has filled in the hole. The sand is flat. Your fears are gone. Buried away somewhere. You can forget them now...."

George was away on his desert island. It was pleasant. It was idyllic. His problems were....

"Now touch your cheek," came the gentle command.

When he obeyed that order he was back to reality. The hypnotist, the room, the fee.

Before George left, the hypnotist gave him some final instructions. "When you feel you want to get rid of all those problems, when they are really bothering you, go up to your bedroom, tell your wife not to let anybody disturb you and go on a trip to your desert island. You know how."

George thanked him and made his way homeward. Again on the top deck of the red bus. But this time he felt a little more confident. He even thought that it might work.

But it didn't.

There was one bit of the desert island fantasy that was wrong. Perhaps the hole was deep. Perhaps it was very, very deep. But it DID have a bottom.

George tried it a few times. Just as instructed. When he

came to the parcels-down-the-hole bit they just wouldn't stay there. They kept bouncing back and landing all around him on the sand. And he was left with a bigger pile of problems than he had started off with. He had consciously gathered them all together into one place.

No. This so-called cure couldn't make him better. It only made the whole situation worse.

George was becoming frantic. Absolutely desperate.

In his search for peace he had found only unrest.

In his search for satisfaction he had only found discontent.

All the options he had tried proved pointless.

All the avenues he had explored led to nowhere.

They were wells without water. Clouds without rain. Hopeless helps.

They had promised everything and delivered nothing.

Where could he go from here?

Wherever now?

What next?

CHAPTER 9
The Despairing Cry

George was at rock bottom.

Life was futile. Absolutely empty. There had to be some reason -some meaning to it all. Something more than the sordid squalor of society as he knew it. Something better that the cheap thrill of passing pleasures. Something beyond the walls of the Hillfoot Bar.

One night he was lying, listless, on the sofa in front of the T.V. It was on, but he didn't see much of it. It was merely a flickering background to misery. He decided to go out to the front door of his house in Glenview Park on the Castlereagh Hills for a breath of fresh air. And a smoke.

Standing there he leaned lightly on the doorpost with one shoulder and lit up a cigarette. There was nobody about. It was one of those moonlit nights when everything was still and starry. It took a few moments for his eyes to adjust from the brightness of the T.V. screen to the unusual beauty of the silent darkness.

As George stood in that doorway he became gradually aware of the unique beauty of that particular night. It was outstanding.

The stars seemed so close that they shone like electric light bulbs. The air was clear. Noises drifted up from the shipyard, far below. Everything was bathed in a silver radiance.

He remained motionless. Mesmerised. Gazing up at the star-studded sky. The cigarette smouldered away between his fingers. Forgotten.

The more he gazed, the more he saw. The more he saw, the more his mind became obsessed by astronomical statistics.

It had interested him to read somewhere that the Sun is over one million times the volume of the Earth, and yet it is only one of a common variety known as "yellow dwarfs." There are other suns out there in other galaxies that are thousands of times bigger than our sun. And there are numberless galaxies.

As our Earth rotates in space at 18 1/2 miles per second and orbits the Sun every 365 1/4 days like a vast clockwork machine, in a million years it is never a second late.

Contemplating the virtually incomprehensible whilst gazing fixedly at the night sky, his heart was pierced with the question, "Where did it all come from George?"

Order like this couldn't be accidental. It didn't happen by chance. It was no big fluke. There must be a Higher Power. An Infinite Intelligence. An Ultimate Potentate. Who or what else could produce and sustain all of this?

As the train of his mind gathered speed on its tracks, other questions suggested themselves, "Do you really believe that there is no God, George? Can you be awestruck by a universe that couldn't create itself and yet deny the existence of a Creator?"

He stopped himself in the mid-stream of contemplation. He applied the brakes to the by now runaway train of his thoughts. As it ground to a halt he was forced to turn introspective. He thought about his thoughts.

When he did this he sensed that something was happening to him.

"Why am I thinking like this?" he asked himself. Although for many rebellious years he had rigorously denied the existence of an Almighty God he had never ever deep down in the secret recesses of his heart actually believed that there wasn't one.

The night was cold. It was winter. It was chilly. It was frosty. But he still stood on, regardless.

Further thoughts were penetrating, and by now perplexing, his mind.

"Do you just die like a dog George? Is that really the end of you?"

He remembered having said that hundreds of times. Thousands perhaps. "You just die like a dog and that's it." It had been good for argument, but he had never truly believed it. After all, mankind had an intelligence that dogs don't have.

He knew that.

George began to realise that he was being made to eat his own words. The bullets that he had fired were boomeranging back and wounding him.

Then like a bolt from the blue, the final shot. The upper cut. The killer punch.

"George, do you reap what you sow?" He had been so convinced all those years ago that there was no God and you don't reap what you sow and that was why he was getting away with everything, or else God was so busy with greater issues, having all those worlds to run, that He hadn't time to notice the evil that he was doing. So what was the point in trying to do good?

Now it was dawning on him. His own personal world was collapsing around his ears.

His mind had gone. His health had gone. His marriage was going.

And this was the reason. The harvest had only been postponed. He was reaping what he had sown. What a fool he had been not to see it!

He was seized by a sense of horror. The thought gripped and penetrated his very soul.

"Whatever a man sows that shall he also reap." The Bible was true after all. And if it was right about this then hell must be a stark reality also. There was a cold shiver running down his spine.

George spent years living through his own self-inflicted hell on earth. Now he was terrified of something different. Something worse. An eternal hell. He firmly believed that there was a place in that hell reserved for him.

Leaning there on the doorpost he could still recollect the crashing as the glass panel of that very door had come up the hall in fragments. Two men had come through it -having smashed it with hobnail boots. They had been coming in for him.

If it hadn't been for his wife who had attacked them with a lead ornament, and the neighbours who had summoned the police, he would have been killed that very night.

There was no doubt about it.

And he would have gone straight to hell. He was convinced of that as well.

From the depths of this reflective tormented mental anguish he cried, "Lord, I know I deserve to go to hell. And I know I have made my bed in this life and I'm going to have to lie in it. I haven't only destroyed my own life. I have destroyed Liz's as well. But Lord, I don't want to go to hell. I know you don't want me to go to hell either. That's why you sent your son to Calvary."

The tears were streaming down his face now. He was trembling. Conviction and realisation were overpowering him.

"All they tell me in Northern Ireland is...," the plea was continuing, "ask God to save you and He will do it. But you know Lord that at times of distress in my life I have done it and it doesn't work for me. It just doesn't work."

George had this idea that something stunning or miraculous should have happened. He had expected to change from Clarke Kent into Superman in a flash. But it hadn't worked out that way.

"Lord, if you are there," the despairing cry went on, "please show me how to get into contact with You. Guide me to a book or a person who will be able to show me what to do.

Lord, if You send me to hell that wouldn't be just. I am pleading with You to show me and whatever You show me I will do it."

When George eventually turned to go back into the house, leaving the beautiful night to its starry stillness, he felt that somehow he had been in touch with God.

It had been faint. It had been far away. But there had been a tiny tug at the end of the line. A nibble. Contact.

But was this just another hopeless help?

Another pointless prayer?

CHAPTER 10
Redundant!

A few weeks later George was standing at the bench in the bacon factory where he worked. He was a supervisor by now and had a well-paid job.

There were other men there too. Working with him and around him. They were all busy. There was general conversation. Normal bacon-boning bustle.

Then up came the foreman and dropped a bombshell.

He shocked the whole squad by breaking the news that the firm was closing and within a couple of months they would all be redundant.

There was a deathly hush. Nobody believed it at first. They had never even dreamed of it. Everything had seemed to be so settled. So stable. So sure.

George had a sense of security, which was now being shattered. It came as a complete surprise to him, but as he started to consider the implications of redundancy, the first thought that came to him was, "Could this have anything to do with the prayer I prayed two or three weeks ago?"

He had asked God to lead him to a book or somebody. Could it be that He was cutting him off from his moorings to do just that?

"No, it couldn't be that," George decided. "But then again, why have I not told any lies since that night? Something must have happened."

George had been a habitual liar. He didn't have to think about telling lies. It came naturally to him. Like breathing. All the other chains were still there. He was cursing, smoking, drinking. But he hadn't felt the need to tell one single lie since his starry encounter with a distant Creator. He cherished that. He valued it. It was always a start. It was such a relief.

Every time George travelled up and down the Castlereagh Road, to and from the city centre in the red bus, something strange happened to him. And it was only since he had heard of his redundancy.

The bus route passed the Hughes Tool Company. A factory on the Castlereagh Road. As George looked out at that factory from the top-deck of the bus, often having to wipe a steamed-up window to do so, something prompted him saying "You are going to be working in there some day."

He didn't even know what they did in it. He imagined that they made huge tools. He thought it was the HUGE TOOL company. But who on earth would want huge tools? Giant screwdrivers and spanners. Colossal chisels. Massive mallets. He could never imagine that.

But he was going to be working in there some day. So the voice-in-his-mind-in-the-bus kept saying.

The last day in the bacon factory finally came.

It was March. It was spring.

It was sad.

The men were still trying to work. But there was nothing much to do. Nothing left to do.

Just a clean up and clear up for close-up.

The foreman came round to say his last goodbyes. It was tough. He was sorry. He liked these men. He asked each man in turn if he had got a job and what he was going to be doing.

Gerry was concerned for them. Every single one of them.

"Well John, have you got another job lined up?" he asked.

"Yes I have," John replied. "I'm starting in a butcher's shop at the Arches on Monday."

"That's great," Gerry said. He turned to Johnny and asked, "And what about you?"

"I've got a wee insurance job Gerry," Johnny was pleased to reply.

He went round them all in turn. Most of them had obtained employment elsewhere.

It had been relatively simple. There were jobs in the land in those days.

George, the supervisor, had been left to the last. "Well George, it's been good to work with you," Gerry began. "Where did you get fixed up?"

The supervisor was on the spot. He didn't tell lies any more. Once he had suspected that God might be guiding him in answer to his prayer he had switched on to automatic pilot. He had taken his hands off the controls of his own life.

But he couldn't say that here.

"I believe I'm going to be working in the Hughes Tool factory," he replied.

"That's great George! When will you be starting?" Gerry was interested.

"Oh I wouldn't have a clue about that," George said. He was slightly embarrassed.

"You have just got an application form in then?" Gerry raised a questioning eyebrow.

"No, I haven't, Gerry," he replied.

Gerry's eyes lit up. He thought he had it all figured out. "You're no fool. You know somebody on the inside who is getting you in."

George resolved within himself that he wasn't going to forfeit this newly found capacity for telling the truth. He said, almost awkwardly, "Well Gerry, if I do know anybody on the inside I'm not aware of it."

This conversation had captured the attention of the whole team. They were interested in each other's welfare. They had worked together for years most of them. Everyone was listening, as Gerry with a quizzical expression on his face asked, "George what do they make in the Hughes Tool factory?"

"To be honest with you Gerry, I haven't got a clue about that either," replied George.

Everybody burst out laughing.

"Oh I see it all now," retorted Gerry in good humour.

"You are trying to take a hand out of the boss on the last day. Is that what it is?"

"No Gerry. That's not it...." George was attempting to explain his obvious lack of direction but he realised that it would be a waste of time. Nobody would understand him.

He gave up.

That weekend George's father came up to visit Liz and he and to see his little grandson Aaron. When he had learned of George's redundancy he asked what to him seemed the next most obvious question, "Where are you starting on Monday son?"

"In Corporation Street da," was George's simple reply.

George Bates senior was furious that a son of his was going on the dole without even looking for a job, and protested, "I could have got you any one of half-a-dozen jobs if you had only told me!"

George tried to explain to his father about his starry night experience and the fact that he was looking to God for guidance.

It wasn't appreciated.

"Have you told anybody else about this outside the family circle?" he inquired.

"You have a wife and child to look after you know!"

"I haven't told anybody daddy," was the sheepish reply.

"Well don't you dare or they'll think you're a nut!" With that he approached George menacingly. Until their faces were almost touching. "They'll think you are the biggest raving lunatic on the streets of Belfast!" he said angrily.

That was his parting shot. He turned sharply and stamped out of the house.

He didn't come back for six months.

And off George went to Corporation Street. Just as he had said he would. On to the dole. He had been earning a good wage in the bacon factory so his dole money was good too. He could live on it easily for six months. And he did. Back and forward to the office he went every week to collect his money and nobody paid much attention to him.

At the end of the six months his dole money would be almost halved. That worried him. He knew that he couldn't support Liz and Aaron on seven pounds a week.

When it came to the final month of the six-month-full-payment-period he became concerned about it.

When it came to the final week of the six-month period and he was still unemployed he became desperate about it.

He thought he was going to have to take up his old position at the controls of his life. He was stuck right out at the end of a limb. Again. Another time.

But before he did anything drastic and before he set off for his final visit of the six-months to the dole office he decided to talk to God about it.

To see if He was going to do something for him.

To give Him a chance to come up with something.

It was a simple contact. Direct.

"Lord if you don't do something for me this week I'm going to have to look out for a job," George prayed. "I have been waiting for You to lead me but You haven't done anything. If You send me to hell someday after me waiting for six months for You to move that wouldn't be just. So please help me. Soon. Now. I ask it in Jesus' Name. Amen."

With that he set off for Corporation Street, hoping that God would move somebody to do something to help him. Very soon.

Seven pounds a week would never be enough.

When his turn came at the reception desk where he always checked in, and collected his money, the girl said, "Mr. Bates you are wanted round at the office."

So George went round to the office. This had to be a move in some direction. He had never been "to the office" before.

"The office" was a very fancy name for it. In actual fact "the office" was a square box-like room. Eight-foot by eight-foot with a hole in the wall.

There was a man looking out of the hole in the wall. Like a chicken peeping out of an egg.

After the necessary introductory formalities had been completed the man-in-the-hole-in-the-wall said, "Mr. Bates, an opportunity has come up for you to go to Felden House Training School."

George nearly fainted.

"Is that Borstal?" he asked.

The training-officer tried hard not to laugh. He saw all sorts. He heard all sorts.

"No, it's not Borstal" he replied. In an off-hand kind of way. Deadpan face. "We realise that you are unemployed through no fault of your own and you had a good record in your previous employment. We are offering you a place at a Government Training School to equip you for a semi-skilled job if you wish."

George's immediate reaction was, "My money's dropping to seven pounds a week and I couldn't live on it."

"Not if you take this course it won't." This bureaucrat had all the answers.

"It will go up ten-bob a week to thirteen pounds ten shillings."

This was a definite opportunity. A chance to become "semi-skilled" and increase his allowance all at one move.

"If that's the case I'll go sir," he replied decisively.

"That's good," the training officer responded. "Very wise. Now what do you want to be?"

"George was stunned. Stumped. He had thirty seconds to decide on his future career and he hadn't the slightest idea of what he wanted to be!

"What DO I want to be?" he thought. "I definitely don't want to be a grocer. I've had enough of that, I can't be a knifeman anymore. There are no jobs at that.

Butcher? Baker? Candlestick maker?

What DO I want to be?

He was aware that the man-in-the-hole-in-the-wall was waiting for his reply. He was tapping with the end of his pen on the ledge in front of him that served as a desk. Patiently waiting.

George was becoming frustrated. And panicky.

He looked around hopefully, searching for inspiration. And he found it. Just beside the pigeonhole, on the George-side of it, there was a poster. There were many posters, but this special one caught George's eye. It read, "Be a CAPSTAN LATHE SETTER OPERATOR."

It was the word CAPSTAN that had attracted his attention. He thought, "That must be a job at the docks. My da always said that there was quare money at the docks."

Pointing to the poster, and trying to conceal his embarrassment, George said, "I wouldn't mind being one of those." He didn't know what it was but he wanted to be one of them anyway!

The cool calm clerk stretched up to look out of his hole-in-the-wall. Just far enough to read the poster that George was pointing at.

"A Capstan Lathe Setter Operator," he read. As he assumed a more comfortable position he gave the relieved George a knowing smile. "Somebody's been tipping you off boy," he said.

George accepted the compliment and filled in a few more forms, still blissfully unaware that he had signed up to train for an engineering job.

Anyone less suited to train as an engineer it would have been difficult to find. This prospective capstan lathe setter operator bent three out of every four nails that he tried to hammer in and bent the lugs of most of the light bulbs he tried to fit into their sockets! He usually managed to screw the top of the toothpaste tube on to the wrong threads!

Whenever he started his course at Felden House Training School the next week and discovered that he was destined to be an engineer, and not a docker, George decided to make the best of it.

He was getting thirteen pounds and ten shillings a week

just for going, and he considered himself well off. Something would turn up!

The course began in the first week of October and was scheduled to last for three months. By that time George would be trained. "Semi-skilled," was what they had called it.

Perhaps he might even land a good job!

During those days on that training course he struggled to be successful. He struggled and was successful.

His struggle was with his hands.

His success was with his head.

He passed all the exams. He learnt all the theory. The theory was all easy enough to learn but when it came to the workshop practice his hands just wouldn't do what his head told them to do! They just wouldn't produce the finished articles! Not the way they looked on the plans or in the textbooks.

But he struggled in another way too. It was mentally. Spiritually really, but he wouldn't recognise the word. It was concerning his relationship with God. The Controller of Creation and Distant Director of his life.

George soon made friends with most of the other young men at Felden during those days. They worked together in the lecture rooms and at the machines during study hours, and spent lunch hours together as well.

Chatting. Smoking. Exchanging jokes and stories. There was one young man, however, and George noticed that there was something different about him. His name was Jim. Jim Magee.

At lunch times when the others were discussing the talent or the trade unions, or some topical issue, Jim slipped away out to his car. George followed him a few times and observed. From a distance.

His observations led him to the conclusion that there must be something seriously wrong in the life of Jim Magee.

Jim used to spend every lunch hour just sitting in his car alone. He had his eyes closed for most of the time. Once or twice George had seen tears shining on his cheeks. A quick flick with a handkerchief wiped these away.

There must be something terrible wrong at home, was George's considered conclusion. Maybe somebody belonging to him is going to die. I wonder is he not getting on well with his wife?

George became concerned for the man-in-the-car. One day the curiosity overcame the caution. He decided to speak to him about it.

Seeing him on his own in a corner of the workshop, George sidled up to him and asked quietly "Jim is there something wrong? Something I could help you with like? I notice you go out and sit in the car on your own every day at dinner time".

Jim smiled at him. "No George there's nothing wrong thanks," he replied. "I just go out to the car to pray."

"To pray! Pray for what?" was the immediate response.

"I pray for a lot of people, and I pray for you every day. I have been saved for a few months now you see, and I would like others to come to know the Lord as well."

That was upsetting to George. He had been curious. He had been concerned. But he hadn't expected that answer. He didn't even like it, and he knew that this man couldn't answer his hard questions.

Since that night on the Castlereagh Hills when he had asked for God's direction, he believed that he had his own special one-to-one relationship with God. But he didn't appreciate anybody else interfering. He didn't need Jim Magee's help or prayers. Or so he thought.

The chap was interested enough in him to pray for him, and that annoyed him.

Then it annoyed him that it annoyed him.

He was still mixed-up. Struggling. Spiritually.

In late November the trainees at Felden began to think of their prospects after the course ended. Employers contacted Felden searching for workers. The successful students were considered lucky. They landed the top jobs.

George was one of the fortunate ones. He had made such good progress on the course that he was awarded one of the first and best jobs to come in.

A top tool room job in Rolls Royce at Dundonald. Pay, £26.00 per week. He was the envy of all his mates. For a whole month.

It came into December. It was coming up to Christmas. Still quite a number of trainees hadn't been placed. They were beginning to worry a little bit.

One day the chief instructor came around the shop floor, spreading good cheer.

"I have been asked to make out a list," he was saying, "another firm wants a number of men."

When he came up to George he was making to go on past. "I'm not putting your name on the list, George," he explained. "You already have a job for January the first in Rolls Royce."

"You're right," was the reply, "but just as a matter of interest where are these jobs?"

"They are in the Hughes Tool Factory." The supervisor was going to walk away. To put somebody else's name on the list.

George stopped him. "The Hughes Tool Factory did you say?" he asked.

"Yes, that's what I said. The Hughes Tool Factory." The supervisor was puzzled.

"Then I want my name on that list," George said.

The supervisor was even more puzzled. "George, this job in the Hughes Tool Factory will only pay £13.00 a week. Half of what you'll be getting in Rolls Royce."

Moving closer to the instructor so that nobody else would hear, George began to explain. "Forget about the money. It doesn't come into it. I am searching for God, and I believe God wants me to work in the Hughes Tool Factory."

He was sincere but almost apologetic in his explanation. Surely any sane thinking person would consider him daft.

It was the instructor's turn to speak quietly. "Son, did you know that I was a Christian?" he asked.

"No I didn't," said George, relieved that he hadn't laughed at him.

"Well I am," he affirmed, "and if you are searching for God I'm not going to stand in your way. If you think you can find God in the Hughes Tool Factory your name will go on the list."

With that he moved on to someone else. And George's name went on the list.

In a few days' time some of the applicants were called for interview.

George was one of those interviewed, and he was offered a job.

He took it.

Turning his back on a job in Rolls Royce at £26.00 per week he accepted one in the Hughes Tool Company at £13.00 per week.

The hunch-in-the-bus had been right.

He was going to be working in the Hughes Tool factory.

Searching for God.

CHAPTER 11
A Helping Hand!

It was early January now. It was cold. It was midwinter.

It was George's first day in the Hughes Tool Company.

The charge-hand was showing him around. The capstan lathe setter operator-to-be was finding out about his new workplace. And it scared him. Stiff.

The six-foot man with the Shankill swagger was explaining it all in a lazy drawl.

"This, son is a drilling machine," he was saying, "and this is a grinder." There were sparks flying all over the place and thin slivers of metal corkscrewed through the air as they shot from machines. Large pieces of steel fell from other machines here and there and clattered to the floor.

And then there was the noise. It was something different. Absolutely deafening.

As he walked timidly beside the gentle giant George thought, "If I don't get sliced in half in this place or blinded by a splinter of red-hot metal, I will most certainly be deaf for the rest of my life."

It was a shock to the system for George. Felden had been like watching performing lions in the circus. Now he was going to be put into the cage with them.

As he was being introduced to the various machines and their functions, George noticed the men who were operating them. By and large however they didn't notice him. They just kept their heads down and worked away. Many of them wore goggles. Some were setting up their machines for the next job.

One or two of them did notice him and gave a friendly nod or wave, and then continued with their work.

"And this is a cutting machine," the voice droned on. George couldn't distinguish one machine from another. They all looked and sounded much the same to him. Big and noisy and frightening. He reckoned that he hadn't been far wrong when he used to think about the Huge Tool factory.

As he rounded a comer between two massive machines with men standing up on them, the "new boy" was taken by surprise as a man in brown overalls, obviously one of the workers, jumped down in front of him.

The workman stuck out his hand and raising his voice above the clamour, said with a smile, "Welcome to the Hughes Tool Company." George was taken aback by this friendly approach and stammered, "Thanks very much."

He took the proferred hand in his and experienced a reaction within his being of having reached his destination.

Like a boat tying up at the quay after a stormy voyage. Like a train chugging slowly in and striking the buffers in the station after a long journey.

He had arrived, he felt.

"And this is a capstan lathe. You'll recognise this one O.K." The guided tour was continuing. The charge-hand was drawing away and the voice was drawling on. The capstan-lathe-setter-operator-to-be followed his leader with a reluctant submission, like a tiny puppy in a big world, being trained to walk-to-heel.

"Excuse me sir," George just had to ask a question. "Who was that man who welcomed me there?"

The man from the Shankill came to a stop. He took off his glasses. Turned and slowly fixed his gaze on the younger man.

In his best Humphrey Bogart-impression-voice he asked, "Are you a Christian kid?"

"No. I'm not. Why?" It seemed a strange question to come from a man like that George thought.

"Well let me give you a bit of friendly advice kid." The charge-hand was becoming the father figure now. "Keep away from that mad fanatic. He'll ram Christianity down your throat, morning, noon and night if he gets the chance. If you give him an inch he will take a mile. Don't say I didn't warn you."

There the conversation ended abruptly, but a wee green light went on in the trainee's mind. A Christian. Surely this can't be accidental? I'm on the right track here.

As they completed their tour of the factory the genial charge-hand was anxious to hear George's reaction to the whole set-up. "Well son, what did you think of all that?" he asked.

"It's a bit frightening," said George. "There seems to be so much to learn."

"Don't worry kid. I think you will learn fast enough. See you in the morning."

With that they parted. It was time to go home.

During that evening he recounted many of his experiences of the day to Liz. And he wondered how he would get on the next day. He doubted if he would ever make a capstan lathe setter operator.

When George did go into the factory, for his first full day's work next morning, he was assigned to the machine of the mad fanatic! The Christian in the brown overalls was to be his mentor! He was delighted!

As he approached the mighty machine the operator was just as friendly as he had been on the previous day.

Stretching out the same welcoming hand to pull George up beside him, he said jokingly, "Jim Moore at your service. Nice to meet you, George."

As the day progressed Jim explained the working of the machine. He would say occasionally "Don't be afraid to ask me any questions you like. Stop me anytime. I would really like to help you if I can." Then he continued to wax eloquent in engineering terms that George didn't understand but he didn't like to admit his ignorance. He tried his best to appear intelligent. And interested. Putting on a front.

"The angle of this cutter can be adjusted up here. And if you want the bore to dwell you set it here." Jim was indicating knobs and levers, wheels and switches in various locations all over the groaning grinding giant. The trainee capstan lathe setter operator nodded now and again in agreement, but in below he was totally bewildered.

Standing up on that mechanical monster he felt like a baby on a bulldozer. Trying to drive it.

"If you want the machine to go in another thirteen-thou you'll have to switch it to manual."

As the engineering crash-course continued George began to wonder, "When's the religious bit going to come? Here's me standing all day with my mouth open, expecting it, and nothing has happened. Like a fledgling waiting for the parent-bird to return with some juicy morsel of food, squawking for it, and it hasn't come yet. When am I going to get this religion shoved down my throat?"

The horn went to end the day. Jim wiped his hands with a cloth. It was home time again. Everybody was jumping down from their machines and making for the locker room.

"Well, George, that's your first full day over. I'll see you in the morning," he was saying. Friendly as ever. "Have you far to go to get home?"

"No Jim, just up the road," was George's reply. "But could I ask you a question please?"

Jim finished folding the cloth and then he hung it on a guardrail at the machine.

"Of course" he said, a little worried. "Is there something I haven't explained properly?"

"No, you've explained everything fully Jim. This is a personal question. Do you mind?"

"No. Not at all." Jim was intrigued. "Go ahead."

"Are you a Christian, Jim?" was the direct question.

"Who told you that?" The expert engineer was visibly shaken. "Who told you that I was a Christian?" he retorted.

"You're ashamed of it Jim!" George was on the offensive now. He didn't like to speak this way to his superior. Especially on the first day of working under him. But it was his disappointment that was doing the talking.

"I am not indeed!" he replied.

"Well I think you are!" George was continuing, "and I'll tell you something else. I don't think much of your Christianity, You're saying to me 'I'll see you in the morning.' I could be in hell in the morning and you never even as much as asked me about my soul."

George was depending on Jim being a Christian. A practising one. The master-of-the-machine was a strong well-built man and could have floored him.

But he didn't.

And he wouldn't.

"Look George," he just reasoned calmly, "someone's been putting it about in this factory that I ram religion at people and I wasn't going to fall into that trap. I have been waiting here all day and praying that you would kick the ball off. Now you have kicked it off and boy are we going to have some game in the morning!"

CHAPTER 12
Contact With God

George had a restless night. He could hardly wait to get into work the next morning. His yearning for work was not caused by any great desire to become the world's best capstan-lathe-setter-operator. It was fired by a curiosity. He wanted to test the mettle of this man Jim Moore. How would he stand up to George's blockbusters?

Morning came. Work began in the Hughes Tool factory. The daily deafening din.

And kick-off came. The game that Jim had promised. The game that George had been looking forward to.

Jim started the machine and explained a few points about its operation to George. Then they started to play.

But the game turned out to be a total flop. If there had been a crowd of spectators they would have been screaming for their money back!

It ended up not so much a game, more a penalty shoot out.

George had all his best shots prepared. He had been using them for years. And winning matches. This was completely different. He felt like an eight-year-old schoolboy in his stiff and shiny new football boots, about a-size and-a-half too big, taking penalty kicks at an England goalkeeper.

As George fired in all his very best shots Jim Moore saved them. He just pushed them over the bar or past the post. That is of course not counting the ones he threw back to George's feet with an encouraging, "Try again boy. Can you not hit me with anything harder than that?"

The day wore on. As they worked they talked. Time passed quickly.

This man was able to handle all George's hard questions. He could explain about the sons of God in Genesis six. Cain and his wife were no problem. Any glaring contradictions in the Bible that he could come up with didn't appear so glaring after Jim Moore had finished.

And he was asking for more questions! "Is that all you have to ask me George?" he said at one stage.

George was tiring. The pace of the game had been too much for him. He had given it all he had. Towards the end of the day George felt like a mud-splattered muscle-cramped player in the second-half of extra-time, and Jim looked as though he had just come out on to the pitch. Fresh as a daisy. Not a trace of mud. Ready for plenty more action.

Before jumping-down-from-the-machine-to-go-home time, George said, "Thank you Jim for all your help."

"Help. What help do you mean, George?" Jim wasn't just sure what he meant.

"I mean all your help in answering my questions about the Bible," was the reply.

Jim looked over at him. "We haven't even started yet George. Are you finished?"

George hadn't finished. Not completely. He had a few more questions that he would like answered.

As the winter days began to lengthen, and the two men continued to work together daily, George learnt many things. He learnt about the workings of the mighty machine. He learnt how to avoid the sparks and the splinters and the falling metal. He learned how to make himself heard above the noise.

And he also learnt about the Bible. And God. And himself.

He used to talk to Liz about it in the evenings. He had told her once that Jim Moore knew more about the Bible than anybody he had ever met. When she saw that he was in the right frame of mind Liz used to ask him, "What were you and Jim talking about today? What was he saying?" She was interested. And George would tell her what they had been discussing. He was interested too.

Jim Moore had won George's confidence and respect. Between talk about angles and boreholes, grinders and gradients, George told him all about his experiences. Jim heard about the desperate struggles. He heard about the suicide attempts. He heard about the starry night experience. He heard about the search after God.

He realised that George was seeking satisfaction. Had been for years.

One day George voiced his inner longing. Straight out. Frank. Direct.

"Jim," he said. "I need to know how to get saved again. I must make real contact with God. I believe that you are the answer to my prayer. God has guided me to you. I have no doubt about that whatsoever."

For once Jim was lost for words. He just didn't know how to respond to that statement. But he didn't have to for George was continuing, with obvious sincerity, "Jim, how can I get saved again?"

"Just take it easy George," was the calm response. George was dying for a drink and looking at a reservoir. He knew that Jim could help him in his search for peace - and his anxiety was beginning to come across.

"Tell me this," the older man wanted to make an accurate diagnosis, "have you ever been saved, George?"

Questions were frustrating. George wanted to be helped not interrogated. He answered nonetheless. "Yes, I was when I was a wee boy," he began, "but that was a long time ago and an awful lot has happened since. I'm not saved now and I want you to tell me how to get saved again."

Some confirmation was required. Bearing in mind what Jim knew of the background. "Are you SURE that you were genuinely saved as a boy?" he asked.

What is he going on about? George wondered. Why doesn't he stop asking so many questions and come up with some answers?

"Yes, I'm definitely sure that I was saved as a child," George affirmed.

"Bear with me for asking, but how can you be so sure?" Jim had yet another question, but his friendly manner and undisguised concern made responding easy.

"Because I have Christ's own word for it and He can't lie. He promised that He wouldn't cast out anybody that came to Him," George said simply.

Jim didn't reply immediately to that confident declaration. He thought for a moment or two and then said, "George, I'm sorry but I have bad news for you."

"What do you mean by that?" George was obviously disappointed. He had never imagined that Jim could be anything other than a proclaimer of good tidings. "What's the bad news?"

"The bad news is that it is impossible for you to be saved again," Jim replied softly.

This came as a shock to a searching soul. George looked over at Jim incredulously. His patient instructor was checking some settings on the machine. "Now Jim, I don't believe that," he began. "I have believed everything that you have told me up until now. But I just don't believe that. Even the dying thief was able to get saved up to the last minute. You're telling me that I'm damned."

"Wait a minute George. Hold on there. I didn't tell you that you were damned." There was something that Jim wanted to clarify for this eager, inquiring spirit. "I have good news for you too." George was glad that he had kept the good news to the end.

"What's that Jim?" he queried. The words all tumbled out in one breath. He was so excited. Hope at last.

"If you were really saved as a boy then you were born again into God's family and you can no more fall out of God's family than you can fall out of your mother's family." That was the simple explanation. That was the good news. All in a nutshell.

The factory thundered on but there was a break in the conversation for a few moments at their machine. George had to consider the implications of that revelation. As he did so the mind boggled.

He turned to Jim at length. "Are you trying to tell me that I'm a Christian?" he asked deliberately and in disbelief. "For if you are Jim, I doubt you haven't been listening to a single thing I have been telling you over the last two or three days. Have you any idea of the things that I have done? Have you no idea at all of the dirty slimy hole that I am slithering out of? And then you're telling me that I'm a Christian! I'm all right!"

Jim beckoned with his hand. He was having bother keeping his tortured trainee from losing his cool. "I'm not telling you that you are all right, George," he replied. Gently corrective. "You are ALL WRONG. You are very far away from God. You need to get right with Him. You are like the prodigal son. Your head is stuck in the pigswill. You need to get back to the Father. I'm simply telling you. God is still your Father."

George quietened. "That's what I want," he said. "I want to get back to the Father. How can I make contact with God?"

The tutor-in-more-ways-than-one was about to vary his approach. Use a Bible story to illustrate his point.

"Ever heard of David the giant-killer?" he asked.

A nod from George meant that he could continue, "Well did you know that he committed adultery and then masterminded the death of the woman's husband?"

"Yes, I know the story," was the reply.

"Do you think that he needed to be saved again?" was the next question.

"Definitely he did." George had no doubt about that one.

The two men were working away and talking away. George could help on the machine now. He listened intently as Jim went on, "That's one thing that even God cannot do. He cannot save you over again. He doesn't have to. He doesn't need to," he explained.

"But let's get back to David. In Psalm 51 we read about him. After confessing his sins to God and pleading for mercy he prayed like this, 'Restore unto me the joy of thy salvation.' That means 'Give me back my joy.' He knew that he hadn't lost his salvation. But he had lost his joy."

That provided George with food for thought. And it provided him with a further topic of conversation with Liz. She was becoming increasingly interested in George's conversations with Jim. And there were many of them.

Any questions that George had they were answered. Anything that Jim thought his apprentice should know, he pointed out to him. Kindly and carefully. When the time was ripe.

On the Friday afternoon just before the hooter-for-home Jim said, "George, would you do something for me over the weekend?"

"I will surely if I can, Jim," was the reply.

"Would you read this little booklet?" was Jim's request. With that he produced a copy of a leaflet called "Safety, Certainty and Enjoyment."

George took the booklet, examined it front and back, flicked through its few pages and then said, "Of course, Jim. If you think it would help me I'll read it over the weekend sometime."

Sunday evening came, the weekend was over, and still George hadn't done his reading homework. Liz said to him as she left the living room, "Are you going to bed, love?"

Not having forgotten the leaflet, or his promise, George replied, "No, you go on up Liz, because my workmate Jim Moore gave me a tract to read and knowing him he will be fasting all weekend and asking me questions about it tomorrow morning." Jim's observant student had noticed that he didn't eat at all regular times, and had been told the reason. "I'll be up as soon as I have it read."

George settled himself on an armchair in the living room by the dying fire and began to read, "Safety, Certainty and Enjoyment." He was starting to read it out of a sense of duty. It was like reading a set novel for an examination. He didn't imagine that there would be much in it to give him any satisfaction. But he had better read it. He had promised.

As he read a few pages into that little book he realised that everything Jim had been telling him about was in it. It brought all the thoughts together and stirred them up in his mind. He was reading avidly now. It was no have-to-hurry-up-and-get-this-finished exercise. He wanted to read it. He craved to know more and more.

Something was happening to him. Tears began to flow freely down his cheeks. Turning round he fell on his knees at the chair. His soul was crying silently to God. The weight of a sense of sin kept pushing him down. From the side of the armchair he slid right down on to the floor. Weeping. Broken. Lying on his stomach on the floor he cried out, remembering David, "Lord I'm a sinner. I confess my sins. Restore unto me the joy of thy salvation."

George was in earnest. He wanted peace. He wanted his joy back. But it didn't return. It was all cold. And dead. There was no contact. The plugs were damp. No spark at all. Nothing fired.

The tears were turning cold on his cheeks. As he wiped them away, a thought shot into his head, "What about Liz? What will you do if she leaves you? If you get right with God she might say "That's the last straw. I'm leaving you George. I can take no more of it"

Lying on the floor, as the room grew colder, and the evening wore on, George made up his mind. He must get into contact with God again. Whatever it cost.

If my mates forsake me - I must get right with God, he decided.

If my father and mother disown me -I must get right with God, he resolved.

Even, and this meant a mighty sacrifice for him, even if my wife leaves me, - STILL I must get right with God, he determined.

At that moment of firm decision to forsake all and find God, it seemed to George that the Cavehill was lifting from his shoulders. The Black Mountain from his back. He was aware that he was now in a position from which he could touch God.

Joy and peace flooded his soul. A joy and peace that he had never known before almost overwhelmed him.

Contact had been made. At last.

But then for a moment his joy was sullied. His newly found peace was disturbed. Like a sudden unexpected, but fierce gust of wind on a tranquil lake.

He became for an instant introverted. Obsessed with himself. What he had done in his lifetime. He imagined himself as the most despicable being in the Universe approaching the Lord Jesus Christ to touch Him with the hands of a beast creeping out of some putrid pit. The nails were long and black and dripping with all the filth and degradation that he had been involved in.

Reason mocked him. It suggested that somebody like him shouldn't even have the face to attempt to touch the Lord. How could he possibly? What brass-necked insolence.

As he began to recoil, realising the logic of that thought, the verse that had meant so much to him as a child came springing and thundering back into his memory, "Him that cometh unto Me I will in no wise cast out."

Reassurance returned.

Of course! That was it!

He was in! He had come to God and he couldn't be thrown out. Or turned away. In no way!

He lay on the floor and hammered it slowly and rhythmically with his fists.

After all those heartbreaking years he had made genuine contact with God!

He was overcome with an unbelievable sense of relief. The prodigal had come back to the Father. He wept for joy. He was safe at last!

Home! Accepted! Forgiven! Clean!

The fire was out when he got up from the floor. But George didn't care about the fire! There was a fire burning in his soul. A fire of peace and joy and love all rolled into one.

Walking about from room to room downstairs he felt so excited. He picked things up and looked at them and set them down again without ever having seen them.

As he revelled in his newly found freedom from the slavery

of sin he was stopped in his tracks. A shock thought struck him. "What was that about the wife?"

He sat down on a chair at the end of the table, cupped his chin in his hands, and thought about it. "Am I going to lose her?" he mused. "Wouldn't it be ironic if I should find peace with God at last, only to lose my family. After all my brave talk. After all my strong determination to get right with God. Will Liz leave me?"

George had to know the answer to that question. And soon.

Jumping up from the chair he rushed out into the hall. And up the stairs. Into the bedroom.

The Reason that had mocked him earlier checked him now. Liz was sleeping peacefully. "Leave it until the morning," whispered Reason. "It will be time enough then."

It seemed sensible enough. Should he? He paused momentarily.

Then George's joy in the Lord on one hand, and his love for his wife on the other and the fear of conflict between the two, spurred him into action. There was no way that this could wait until the morning.

Moving over beside her, George shook Liz gently on the shoulder. Nothing happened. He must get through to her. He shook her more vigorously. She began to stir.

"I have something to tell you," he said softly. This didn't have the desired effect. He shook her even more vigorously. Almost violently.

Liz sat bolt upright.

"Liz, I have something to tell you! I have something to tell you!" In his desire to be urgent, he had almost forgotten that he needed to be gentle. Or quiet. He was speaking loudly. And quickly.

Having been awakened so suddenly Liz instinctively thought that something terrible had happened to somebody. A look of fear crossed her face.

"Oh George is it the child?" she cried. "Is it my mammy? What has happened? Oh tell me! Tell me quickly!"

It was a funny sort of half-sleeping, half-crying, half-mourning kind of exclamation.

George put his arm round her. He hadn't meant to cause her this distress.

Looking down at her, he spoke again. Tenderly this time. "Calm down now Liz. Calm down. Everything is all right" he assured her. "I just need to talk to you. That's all."

Liz was now sitting up in bed, wide-awake. She didn't know what to expect. She shivered once or twice. Deep uncontrollable single shivers. Part-shock-part-fear-part-cold.

Her profoundly happy, but still slightly apprehensive husband began, "You know, Liz, I have been telling you about talking to Jim Moore in the factory. How we talk about God and the Bible and all. And you know how that I don't believe in lukewarm half-hearted Christianity. Either you are on the Lord's side or you're not. I can't stand hypocrites. You know that Liz...."

He paused to look down at her again. To gauge her reaction. How was he getting along so far? How was she taking it?

Before he could resume, Liz butted in, "What is it you want to tell me George?"

She was impatient. She had been wakened up in the middle of the night to hear something vitally important and she hadn't heard anything yet that she didn't already know!

Feeling that he had to put her into the picture straight away he went right to the point. Directly and without further preamble. "Liz, I have got right with God tonight and I am sure that He has forgiven me," he continued in a strong even voice. "But before I could find that inner peace I had to promise God that no matter who left me I would go on with Him."

At that moment Liz began to wail. George was startled. Frightened almost. He had never seen her like this before. He had never heard anything like this before.

She just sat there huddled up in the bed and wailed. It

seemed to her bewildered husband that she had opened her mouth and had lost the power to close it. Her voice came in one long high-pitched monotone. A sustained shriek.

As he gazed at her in awestruck silence, George was gripped with a sense of despair. His stomach seemed to hit the bedroom floor. This was it! She was going to leave him.

Not knowing what to say, or how to react to this outburst he asked anxiously, "Liz, what's the matter? What's wrong?"

There was no reply. She was crying so much that she couldn't talk. George waited a few more moments and Liz began to quieten down. The wailing turned to weeping. The shrieking to sobbing. But it didn't stop.

And still she didn't speak.

George paced up and down the room. Beside the bed. There wasn't much space but he used every inch that he could find. Eventually, when he could bear it no longer, he went round to his own side of the bed. Catching the pink eiderdown by the corner he threw it back, and sat down beside Liz.

Reaching over he caught her by both shoulders, turned her around so that he could see her face, and shook her again. He was in a panic. What did all this mean?

"Put me out of my misery, Liz," he begged. "Tell me what's the matter!"

Tears were flowing freely down her red-with-the-cold-and-flushed-with-excitement cheeks. Like a shallow summer stream clinging to a sandstone rock face in a gentle waterfall.

"Oh George," she said at last through her tears. "I got saved on Friday night and I was afraid to tell you in case you would throw me and the child out onto the street!"

So that was it! That was what all the crying and wailing was about!

They were tears of joy! But she just couldn't believe it!

And neither could George! It was like an electric shock to him! He was numbed by joy. Speechless with ecstasy. Over the moon.

When the power to think and speak returned, George's immediate response was a phrase he had used often in his tell-a-story-in-the-bar-days. "Liz, you're kiddin'," he said, still astounded.

This couldn't, couldn't possibly be true! God had put His Mighty Hand on both of them. Unknown to one another!

"No George I'm not kiddin'. I mean it. I got saved on Friday night!" The joy of confession had given her further confidence and her soul was flooded with peace.

This was a time for celebration. Jumping up from where he was sitting on the edge of the bed, George ran round to the other side and half-pulled Liz out of the bed.

She was probably going to get up anyway.

He hugged her!

He kissed her!

He danced round the room with her!

They bumped into the dressing table and all the knick-knacks rattled and settled.

They fell on their knees beside the bed and poured out their hearts to the Lord. Sometimes one at a time -and sometimes both at once!

They weren't long prayers. But they were sincere! They were from overflowing thankful hearts!

George. And Liz. And God. And each one was in real, living, exciting contact with the other two!

"Dear God, thank you for saving us!" they said.

"Thank you Lord for Calvary!" they said.

"We want to love You and serve You all of our lives." they said.

"Lord we don't deserve it! But Thank you! Thank you! Thank you!" they said. Then they got into bed.

Then they couldn't sleep!

They were so, so happy!

"Do you feel the way I feel, Liz?" George asked once.

"I don't know whether I feel the way you feel or not!" she replied. "But I can tell you this. If you feel the way I feel, you'll feel great!"

"Let's praise the Lord again!" George exclaimed.

So out of bed they got again. Down on their knees at the side of the bed. Again.

Praising and thanking God for His love.

And their joy.

And His patience.

And their satisfaction.

And His protection.

And their unity.

And His peace.

Then they clambered into bed again. Only to rise ten or fifteen minutes later and repeat the whole procedure.

This continued for the remainder of the night.

Dances of delight. Pirouettes of praise. Unbelievable bliss!

The pink eiderdown was on and off the bed more times than they could count!

As morning approached, the wonders of the previous weeks unfolded to their delighted souls.

George had been carrying home the seeds of salvation from the Hughes Tool Factory and planting them in Liz's mind. The soil of her soul had been both receptive and fertile. And had borne fruit. An hundredfold.

God had worked a modern miracle!

They were the proof!

And they intended to prove it to others!

CHAPTER 13

This Is For Real

Rising for work that Monday morning had posed no problem. George had been up for half of the night anyway, and with the sense of peace and joy that had flooded his soul he just couldn't wait to tell his workmates about it.

Many of them were Christians.

All of them would be thrilled he was sure.

Especially Jim.

What would he say? What would he think?

And what a surprise!

George had not only to tell them about himself. But his wife as well! That was the big bonus! The icing on the cake.

But between getting-up time and getting-out time Liz and he had to go through a well rehearsed, tested and tried, early morning routine. All out-to-work families have their own. Practised and polished to perfection.

Turns in the bathroom. Breakfast at the bench. Lunches to be prepared. Four minutes to the bus stop.

Part of the ritual in the Bates' household was Liz' preparation for George's departure.

Every morning she set out on the mantelpiece, at the left-hand side beside the fan-shaped clock, his clean handkerchief, his packet of cigarettes, his lighter and his "piece".

Four items. In their place. Every morning without fail, sitting waiting for George to pick them up. That was the last movement in the symphony.

On that marvellous Monday as he was pulling on his overcoat to go out, Liz reminded him, "Don' t forget your fags and your piece, love."

She was happy and aglow with a newly found delight. But she hadn't expected anything to change.

George stepped over to the fireplace. Lifting his hanky from the mantelpiece he put it into his left-hand pocket. Then he slipped his lunch into the right-hand pocket of his overcoat.

That left only the cigarettes and the lighter. He reached out his hand, sub-consciously almost, to put them into his pockets as well. But the hand that had performed this so-simple-task so-easily so-often now seemed to be operated by an outside force. Like a mechanical grab on a digger. He picked up the cigarettes from the left-hand side of the mantelpiece and placed them carefully over on the right-hand side!

Turning his back on both them and the lighter he walked towards the door out into the hall. To go to his work.

Liz was puzzled. She said to him, "What are you doing George?'

That was a hard question to answer. Although he didn't understand it, George was now totally switched over to automatic pilot. He was under new management.

Looking down at his caring wife he replied, "Liz don't even speak. I don't know what I'm doing."

With that he left the house to go to the Hughes Tool Factory. To tell genuine Jim and his praying friends the wonderful news.

It would be the-morning-after-the-night-before. With a difference.

On arrival on the shop floor an explanation proved to be unnecessary.

Jim took one look at George and asked, almost anticipating the answer, "What has happened to you?"

The whole story gushed out. Good news of great joy. A torrent of delight. Like a dam bursting. Lock gates opening.

The sheer joy on his face radiated the relief in his soul as George began to recount to his instructor-friend the events of the night before.

The reading. The praying. The crying.
The resolve. The peace. The satisfaction.
His contact with God.
Liz. And her story. Her shock. Her salvation.
Their contact with God.

The master-machine-minder couldn't wait for George to finish. His pupil was excited. Exuberant. He could have talked all morning about his peace at last. And Jim could have listened.

But there were others who would want to hear this news. It had to be shared. Immediately grabbing George by the elbow he marched him round the factory. Like the proud owner of the Supreme Champion at the Balmoral Show.

Every Christian in the Hughes Tool Factory heard about it.

"Wait to you hear this!" Jim would say.

"Go on George tell them about it!" he would say. Men jumped down from their machines. Beckoned to others across the shop floor. They grouped around George.

He could tell them everything they wanted to know. Without even opening his mouth.

They just had to look at him. He was shining. His joy was infectious. His peace was obvious.

He talked anyway. For he wanted to tell them about it. He told them what he had been telling Jim. And more. As he spoke to different groups the whole story of the night before was revealed. He was pleased that they were so pleased. This was an answer to prayer. For Jim. And all of them.

Jim had been telling them about George.

And they had been telling God about George.

Now George had come to tell them about God.

Mighty. Marvellous. Miraculous.

The gentle giant with the Shankill swagger looked over at one of these joyful clusters. He stretched up and out his arm in a friendly fashion. The hand held the pipe that was a part of his person. He always sucked it but seldom smoked it!

Nodding his head with a resigned smile, he said, "I warned you. Didn't I?!"

It was a good-natured remark and the returned prodigal just waved over and laughed back. His Christian workmates had been in the process of inviting him to join them at lunchtimes. At a prayer meeting. A number of them met together briefly to pray and read the Bible. So he had been interested to find out.

For George this was a new experience. An exciting one. As the days passed he and Liz were rejoicing in the Lord and learning more and more about the living reality of having God in their lives. And their home. And their marriage.

And he was revelling in his contact with God. At home and at work.

He had accepted his workmates' invitation to the lunchtime prayer session. He had been happy to. He enjoyed hearing these men pray. They were in touch with God. He realised that. But he didn't pray out loud. He couldn't. He was afraid. A paralysing fear was shackling his soul.

It was a fear of the past. A fear of his blaspheming cursing tongue.

A voice nagged at him. Restraining him. "You think you can control your tongue now," it kept saying. Taunting him. "But you can't. You have only hit upon a hidden vein of will power that you didn't know you had. Just open your mouth in one of these prayer meetings and you are going to make an awful fool of yourself. You are going to end up with a shocking red face. It will all come out. A mouthful of lovely language. What will all these holy Christian boys think of you then?

Things had changed at home as well. Totally. So many unexpected blessings.

George spent a lot more evenings at home now. With Liz and Aaron. On one such evening he was sitting by the fire listening to some home-recorded tapes on a reel-to-reel tape-recorder, half the size of a suitcase, and bang up to date.

They were a musical family and loved to sing. And record their singing to play all over again.

George listened idly as his little son Aaron sang in his tuneful childish voice, the Dubliners hit,

"You're drunk, you're drunk
You silly old fool"

He had picked up all the barroom ballads from his mum and dad.

The tape whirred on with family recollections and trivia. George smiled and nodded to himself now and then as pleasant memories spilt out and tumbled over in his mind.

It was recent family history.

It was cosy. Comforting. Interesting.

Suddenly his heart skipped a beat. He sat up straight in the armchair.

Aaron was singing again. On the same tape.

"Jesus loves me, this I know
For the Bible tells me so."

It was the same child. Same voice. Different words.

Gradually George was beginning to appreciate the far-reaching effects of his return to living contact with his long-suffering Creator. And Liz's conversion.

It had touched their lives. Their home. Their marriage.

Even their little son.

As those blissful learning-loving days added up into months, George had been gaining in confidence in the Hughes Tool Factory. Almost unknown to himself it had seemed, as there was so much else going on. And the management of the Hughes Tool Factory had demonstrated its confidence in him. By placing him in charge of his own machine. A capstan lathe.

He had made it! He wasn't a docker. He was an engineer. A fully-fledged capstan lathe setter operator.

In the midst of the bustle of one of those busy noisy working days George lifted a spanner to tighten a nut. He was setting up his machine for another new job. There is a tendency for the inexperienced to over tighten. Just to make sure. Give it that last final face-flushing twist!

As he did so, straining every muscle to make sure that it wouldn't move another millimetre, the spanner slipped from the nut. It shot forward, ripping a ragged gash in the knuckle of his other hand which had been gripping tightly on to a bar in front of him.

Blood spurted up into the air. Like a hot-red spring. Running down the back of his hand it stopped at the cuff of his overall. Staining it scarlet.

Pain penetrated every fibre of his body.

If ever there was an excuse for a spontaneous ripper, this was it!

But it didn't come. God was in control. He had taken over the tongue. Become Master of the mouth. As well as everything else.

When the realisation of the fact that it wasn't just a hidden vein of will power after all began to register in his mind, George just had to give God the glory. He must!

Opening his mouth to its widest extremity he emitted a shriek of "Hallelujah! Praise the Lord!" It was so loud that it could be heard by all his workmates on adjacent machines. Even above the constant ear-splitting din of the factory floor.

Heads turned in the direction of the triumphant yell. In consternation.

What they had observed was baffling. It seemed rather incongruous to see somebody clasping one blood-stained hand with another, the persistent blood attempting to force its way through the fingers of the protecting hand -and shouting "Hallelujah!"

Now the praying out loud could begin. And it did from that very day. Without fear.

A new life had begun for George and Liz. They knew now that they didn't have to reap what they had sown. And they weren't going to either. Ever. For Another had reaped the horrible harvest on their behalf. At Calvary.

And they were free. Forgiven. Pardoned. Free forever. The chains had snapped. The fetters of iron had cracked. They were released from their bondage.

The television had been part and parcel of the life of their home for many years. It was seldom off. It was this perpetual intrusion of the outside world into their living room that fired George with a burning desire to tell everybody else about the mighty things that God could do for them as well.

It was a Sunday evening. A televised church service. The camera had been positioned in the gallery of some historic cathedral and was being panned over the congregation involved in liturgical worship.

He looked at the screen and said, with a sense of concern, "Liz, look at that. All those lovely people in their moral uprightness. So many of them going through the motions of pretending that they are in touch with God. They haven't a clue, through no fault of their own probably, that they don't have to pretend. They just don' t know what God has revealed to us."

He looked away from her, back to the T.V., and back to Liz, again. She was waiting for more. She knew George, and she knew he hadn't finished. And she was right. He hadn't

Springing to his feet he took two giant steps across the floor. He flung his arms forward and stretched out his hands in one flowing gesture.

"Liz, we have to tell them that there's more to live for than this," he continued earnestly. "What we have found is more than just an insurance cover note to keep us out of hell. More than ritualistic religion.

We have to tell everybody. Moral straight up and down people like them on the T. V. And the dregs of society as well.

About the new life that we have found.

Praise God! This is for real!"

CHAPTER 14
Their Eyes Were Opened

This wonderful new landscape of life wasn't always and altogether bathed in sunshine. There were shadows cast by past desires. Old habits die hard.

George hadn't turned from Clarke Kent into Superman overnight. True enough.

His immediate problem was the cigarettes. The fags.

He had been smoking sixty a day. From sixty-a-day to none-a-day was a big jump. A shock to the system. Withdrawal symptoms were worst after a meal or a cup of tea.

Sitting in the canteen of the Hughes Tool Factory each day proved to be a real testing-time. When they had finished their lunch many of his workmates sat around, chatting and smoking. Ash was flicked into saucers or plates. Smoke drifted lazily up into the air. As the atmosphere became permeated with cigarette smoke George found himself gasping to inhale the stale second-system smoke.

Jim was talking to him across the table. George was looking past him. He was gazing longingly at a group of men in the background who were smoking and yarning.

Looking directly at him, Jim said pointedly, "I'm not getting through to you at all today, George. You're not listening to a word I'm saying. What's wrong with you anyway?"

"Jim, the Devil is really tempting me with the smell of these cigarettes. I'd love a smoke," was the honest reply.

Of course! Jim was secretly annoyed at himself. He should have realised that the smoke in the canteen would have been a problem to George. A former chain-smoker. Someone for whom cigarettes had been a drug. A way of life. He should have anticipated it!

Jumping up from his seat, he reached across and grabbed George by the elbow, "Come on!" he commanded, "Get up! We're getting out of here!"

He marched George about. Again. Holding him by the elbow again, as he had done before. Only this time it was like a fireman guiding a choking child from imminent danger in a smoke filled building.

Heads were turned in their direction and faces showed expressions of mild amusement as George was directed, gently but firmly, to the outside door.

They stepped outside. A steady breeze was blowing, causing leaves and scraps of paper to play endless tig with each other round the yard.

"Here now George," Jim instructed. "Take a few deep breaths of that. That's God's good fresh air!"

George complied. And as he stood there breathing deeply, filling his lungs with "God's good fresh air," Jim was continuing with yet another explanation. Something else that his previously prodigal pupil ought to know.

"Although salvation is an instantaneous thing, possessing the land takes time. God will help you George," he was saying. Jim was always encouraging. Reassuring. Helpful. "Ask Him. Keep asking Him. Victory will come."

George nodded in assent but something within him kept wondering if victory would ever come. The craving was so strong.

They went back inside. It was time to return to their machines.

Midway through the afternoon George was almost overcome by the desire for the familiar soothing effect of a smoke. A drag at a fag. If only he had one!

A voice, an instinct, seemed to be saying to him, "Leave your machine now and go to the toilets. There will be somebody there with one they could give you."

The gales of temptation were howling now. In all their

fury. The one-time heavy smoker was almost overwhelmed. Capsized. Swamped. Sunk. He stood at the machine with his head bowed.

The factory thundered and groaned, rattled and whistled all around him.

"God, I believe in the reality of your Word. I need You to help me." He had glanced around furtively to make sure nobody was watching. Now he was praying fervently. Only God could hear him above the racket.

"This is the acid test," he went on. "God You know that I don't believe in fairies. Fairies would be no good to a boy like me. But I do believe in You. I need Your power to help me right now. If You don't deliver me from this desire for a cigarette I'm sorry but I'm going to have to get out of here and go for a smoke. Somewhere. Somehow. Please help me God. Amen."

It was one of those passionate prayers that George had prayed on previous occasions. A my-back's-against-the-wall and I'm-at-the-end-of-my-tether-type-prayer.

But he didn't expect the answer that he received. He thought that he was down. And out. He was just going under for the third time. Spluttering. Sinking. Drowning.

God delivered him again. Mightily. Permanently. Powerfully.

George remained at his machine. A sense of inward contentment flooded his soul. He was able to concentrate on his work again.

And from that day until now he has never again had an urge to smoke. It had gone. For good.

Two months of rapid Christian growth had elapsed between the time of George's return to the Lord and one Monday morning when he was helping Jim on the big machine. He loved to get over there because although he knew most things about the operation of the machine, he was daily discovering new gems about the operations of God. A high percentage of what he knew about the dealings of God in relation to mankind he either learnt from, or shared with, his spiritual friend and guide, Jim Moore.

They were recounting the events of the weekend past. George had a problem. A concerned curiosity.

As they worked away, he asked his question. "Jim, tell me this. What do Christians do with themselves on Saturday nights? It seems to me that they must all hibernate. Like bats. Or hedgehogs or something."

Further explanation was to reveal the need for the question. And the comment. "You see, my father called on Saturday afternoon at our house to see if Liz and I wanted to go out anywhere. He and my mum offered to baby-sit. Saturday night has always been our big night out. He asked if there was anything we really wanted to do. There was. One thing. I said to him, 'Daddy, I would love to go to a Christian meeting.' He asked me where it was, Jim, and I hadn't a clue. So I just said, "I'm not sure. But I would like to go to one somewhere. There must be dozens of them."

George thought that while half-the-world was in the boozers and the dance halls all the Christians must be in the churches.

'Son, I'll take you. Don't you worry about it. We'll find one somewhere,' my father had promised me, before arranging to come back in the evening.

Jim was working away and listening intently. It was intriguing this. He kept wondering what the outcome would be.

George was in full flow. "So Liz and I got all dressed up in our Saturday night regalia. Father came up when he said he would and we piled into his car and toured this city Jim. We were looking for a Christian meeting. But we found nothing but closed doors! All the churches were shut! We tried the Baptists. We tried the Brethren halls. We even tried the Ulster Hall. We thought there might be some sort of a do on in it, but it was shut too! We tried everywhere we could think of. We drove around for half the evening and found nowhere open. We had to go home again Jim. All dressed up and literally nowhere to go! And we never found a Christian meeting. Open."

As he stopped to draw breath, George looked over to see how his tutor was taking all of this. He was almost finished. His final question was to be a repeat of his first. A restatement for re-emphasis, "I'm asking you again Jim. What DO Christians do with themselves on Saturday nights?"

It was a moment or two before Jim replied. He was disappointed for George. He felt that he must clarify the situation. And apologise on behalf of the Christians in the city of Belfast. Knowing that he could leave the machine to rumble on unattended for a few minutes, he turned round fully to face George, who was standing patiently waiting for an answer.

"The Christians are probably preparing for Sunday, George. You see, that's their big day," he began. "It's a pity you didn't go to the Coalmen's Mission though. It's packed out on Saturday nights." Then by way of continuing the conversation, Jim asked in his usual friendly fashion, "What would you normally have done on a Saturday night? Before you got back to the Lord I mean."

"Oh I always reserved Saturday nights for going out for a drink with my father-in-law, John Miskelly," was George's offhand reply.

At that moment Jim looked as though a bolt of lightning had struck him.

Looking at George with a strange incredulous expression he asked sharply, "Who? Who did you say? Who was that you were drinking with?"

"John Miskelly," George said.

"Is that the John Miskelly who worked in the shipyard?" Jim was persistent and deadly serious.

"Yes," George replied, "That's him. He's my father-in-law. Do you know him?"

Jim answered George's question by asking another one of his own. "You're not the son-in-law that used to sit in the Hillfoot Bar with him on a Saturday night are you?"

"I am, Jim," George continued, surprised that Jim had ever even heard of the Hillfoot Bar.

Jim doubled over. He couldn't speak. He was like a sportsman winded on the playing field. Like a soldier wounded on the battlefield. Holding his stomach, and still bent double, he clambered down from the machine. He shuffled across to a nearby drinking fountain and bent down over it. Pretending to take a drink.

George followed him down. He was really worried. His friend must have taken a sudden attack of something serious. Maybe it was a cardiac arrest.

Bending down beside his gasping tutor he inquired anxiously, "Will I get help Jim? Are you sick?"

Jim straightened up a little. "No. Don't attract attention. I'll be O.K. I'm just winded."

When he had regained his composure he stood with his back against the wall beside the drinking fountain. Just to make sure that there could be no mistake he reiterated, "Let me get this right, George. Are you the man that sat in the Hillfoot Bar on a Saturday night arming your father-in-law with the questions to fire at the Christian in the shipyard?"

Now it was George's turn to be astonished. "I am," he confessed meekly. "But how did you know about that?" His heart was racing and his breath was coming in short gasps.

"I know because I am the one that you were preparing the questions for." Jim's voice was trembling with excitement. "I am the Christian fella from the shipyard. I didn't know your name but I have been praying earnestly every day for three years that God would smash John Miskelly's rebellious son-in-law and bring him to Christ."

Tears welled up in Jim's eyes as he continued, "Do you mean to tell me that God has brought you through redundancy. Through six months on the dole-queue. Through Felden House Training School. Into the Hughes Tool Factory and right on to my machine. I have pointed you back to Christ and I didn't even know who you were!"

The two men, tutor and trainee, one a spiritual giant the other a spiritual green-horn, stood gazing at each other in shocked amazement. They were speechless. They were overcome as they pondered their past.

They were beset by a sense of awe and wonder when they realised that an Invisible Hand had reached out of Eternity into Time and had been manipulating their lives. Moving them about from place to place. Precisely. Strategically. Like pieces on a chessboard.

They were humbled but pleased to be part of a Divine Master Plan.

And the Controlling Hand had nail scars in it!

CHAPTER 15
The Tax Rebate

Much time had been wasted. There was a lot of ground to make up.

George had emerged, blinking, from the total darkness of the slavery of sin, into the marvellous light of freedom with God. As his eyes adjusted to the light of liberty he realised that there was much to see. And hear. And experience. And express.

Now that all the obstacles had been removed and the Direct-Link-to-Heaven was open twenty-four-hours-a-day he had a lot that he wanted to say!

He had so much praying and praising to do! How he enjoyed those times! His greatest delight was to come home in the evenings from the hustle of the Hughes Tool Factory, chat to Liz and Aaron over and after tea, and then go upstairs and shut himself off with God. For hours at a time!

George was always careful to prepare himself well for these Divine appointments. He would wash off the grime from his work, change his clothes and comb his hair before going upstairs.

One evening he was surveying himself in the mirror above the mantelpiece. Liz was sitting on the sofa, knitting, and watching him out of the corner of her eye. He was just putting the final touches to a hair-combing session, stroking the last stray into place, when she asked him, "George, are you going out somewhere?"

"No I'm not Liz," was the reply. "I'm going' upstairs to pray."

"I didn't think you would need to dickey yourself all up like that to go up the stairs," Liz remarked, with a quiet laugh. She meant no harm.

George didn't like to think that he was being laughed at. Not by Liz, and certainly not in relation to his vital, precious, contact with God.

"Well Liz, it's like this." he explained. "If I was invited down to the City Hall or somewhere else to meet somebody really important I would dress myself up in my very best. Is it not much more essential that I dress myself up to meet the King of Kings?"

Liz said no more. She smiled and nodded. Only the click of the needles and the tick of the clock broke the silence. He was right, and she knew it. Contact with God meant much to both of them.

George spent many evenings praying and praising. He knelt at a chair or a bedside and poured out his grateful heart to God.

He prayed for two or three hours at a stretch. Saying, perhaps a thousand times over, "Lord, I love You," or 'Thank you Lord for Calvary."

His gratitude to God was unceasing. As he reflected on his past life, he was so thankful to God for all His patience and longsuffering. All His mercy and His grace. But one thing began to bother him. To bug him. It began to get to him.

What about all those people that he had cheated? Stolen from. He had betrayed their trust. There must be something that he could do for them. But what? Or how?

There was old Markey Moore and his sister. There were shopkeepers from whom he had stolen many things. Not once or twice. But often. Shoplifting had been a game that he had played. A battle of wits. He had devised his own straight-into-the-pocket profit-sharing scheme with his employers. Without their knowledge, of course!

The task of making restitution was so vast that it seemed almost impossible. He had stolen so much from so many for so long! Yet the conviction to repay was equally strong. And growing stronger.

It was becoming an obsession with him. It was even beginning to cloud his happiness. If he couldn't repay everything to everybody he could at least pay something to somebody. That is if he had the something.

One evening as he was praying George brought it to God. "Please God, I know that You want me to pay these people back," was his petition. "But You know that I can't. I just haven't enough. In Your might and power please send me the money to do it. I ask it in Jesus' Name. Amen."

And there he left it. With God.

A few days later Liz and he were chatting over breakfast. More correctly George was having breakfast. Liz was buzzing about. Watching toast, making his "piece", attending to Aaron. But she was never too busy to talk. Especially when the point of the exercise was to "touch up" her husband for something she wanted.

"George, I wish I had a new basket for my groceries." She dropped the opening remark quite casually. As though she had just thought of it! "The one I have is done. And anyway it's not nearly big enough."

Between bites of his toast, sips of his tea and glances at his watch, George nodded. And grunted. And responded as enthusiastically as he could at twenty-to-eight in the morning. "The Lord will look after that in His own time. Don't worry, love." He wasn't really terribly concerned about shopping-baskets at breakfast time.

After having picked up his hanky and his "piece" he set out for the Hughes Tool Factory.

It had been a pretty ordinary day at work. But it was a special day at home. Or so Liz thought.

When George arrived home that evening Liz met him at the door. She was flushed with excitement. Her face was glowing and her eyes were like saucers. "George you will never believe it!" she exclaimed.

"I'll never believe what Liz!" George replied. "What has happened?" Liz led the way into the living room. "Sit down there a minute George, till I tell you. I want to show you something."

It must be something extra-special to send Liz into ecstasies like this. He seated himself on the sofa as instructed. And waited. He didn't even take off his coat.

Stepping over to the fireplace, Liz produced a piece of paper from behind the clock. She flourished it before her puzzled husband, "Look, George. You have got an income tax rebate!"

George glanced down at the piece of paper, which Liz had placed below his nose, and then permitted him to take into his hand.

She was right. It was an income tax rebate. It was the first income tax rebate that he had ever received. And George had never imagined that he would ever receive as much money at one go! It seemed like a fortune to him! And to Liz.

As he sat transfixed, gazing at the rebate cheque, Liz was strutting about. From the living room into the kitchen. And back. While she walked, still she talked. "I'm going to be able to get that shopping-basket I was talking about after all, George" she was saying. "God has provided the money like you said. There's more than enough. I'm sure you could buy a dozen shopping-baskets with that!"

George's heart sank. He was going to have to disappoint her. And he hated doing that.

"Liz come here a minute, love," he beckoned.

She sat down beside him on the sofa. And she read his face. Something was the matter. "What's wrong George?" she asked. How could there be anything wrong with anybody sitting holding a cheque like that? She wondered.

George took her hand. A time for tenderness. When he spoke, it was softly. "You know I wouldn't begrudge you your bag, Liz. You buy whatever you like with that money. But I have to tell you before God that that's not what it's for. I have been asking God to send me the money to make good some of the wrong that I've done. I don't believe that this is any accident, but I'm leaving it entirely with you."

When Liz sensed the conviction and urgency in the tone of her husband's voice she knew what she must -or mustn't do. She couldn't hold back even the price of a shopping-basket from God.

Turning round to look right over at him, she said without hesitation or even the slightest hint of disappointment, "You do what God has told you to do, George. I'll not stand in your way."

She was right behind him all the way. If it meant doing anything for God. He had done so much for them.

So when he had an afternoon off, George set out to begin the mammoth task of compensating for some of the wrong that he had done. Paying back some of the money. Distributing the income tax rebate.

His first object was to find Markey Moore - and make things right with him,

As they were standing in the hall just before George set out, he was counting the money. A fistful of five-pound notes. Liz was watching him. What would all that not buy? Yet she didn't complain. But one thought did come to her.

Had done before, but she hadn't voiced it until now, "What happens if he takes you round to the police station?"

"I have been wondering about that myself," was the concerned reply. "I don't know what I'll do. But I want you and Aaron to stay here and pray that he doesn't. I must find him anyway, if I possibly can."

He had no trouble finding the house. He remembered it only too well. In a little street off the Beersbridge Road. Near Elmgrove School.

As he knocked the door George wondered to himself, "Could old Markey still be alive? Does he still live here?"

He hadn't long to wait for the answers. "Yes, Markey Moore does still live here," the woman who answered the door said in response to his query. "But he's not in at the minute. He goes out every day for a walk."

"Have you any idea where he goes for his walks?" George asked.

"He's very fond of the Ormeau Park," the friendly woman, who George had never met before, continued. "But really he could be anywhere. He walks all over the place."

After he had thanked her and left the door George decided to try the Ormeau Park first. It would be easier to find Markey in the Ormeau Park than in "anywhere". It would be more difficult to search.

It was a dull evening. A drizzle that drenches slowly but surely was falling on the city. And George didn't find Markey Moore in the Ormeau Park. He walked all through it. Covering each path once, and some of them twice.

As the darkness of the night threatened to envelop the darkness of the day he decided to walk home.

Perhaps this was a stupid idea after all. Perhaps it wasn't what God wanted at all. Maybe they should just keep the money?

As he walked up the Castlereagh Road in the dusk he was frustrated. He had wanted to do what he thought to be right. He had the best of good intentions. Now he was dispirited. Disappointed. Dejected.

George had by now given up all hope of finding Markey Moore that day. He had become so totally preoccupied with his musings that he had caught up with the old man before he was actually aware of it.

There was an old man shuffling in front of him. He was dressed in a well-worn dark overcoat, a muffler and a cap. He was bowlegged this old man, and walked with a kind of a rolling gait. Like a boat gently swaying on a swelling tide. That was him! It was Markey Moore! There was no mistaking that muffler! Or that walk!

The last thing that George wanted to do was to frighten him. So he caught up with him without running, and after he had half-passed him he turned round and asked gently, "You're Markey Moore. Aren't you?"

"Yes I am," the old man replied. He was a bit suspicious. Naturally.

It was important that he be put at ease as soon as possible, so George went on quickly, "You probably don't remember who I am, but I'm George Bates. I used to deliver the messages to your house years ago. But I have been looking for you. Let me tell you why."

Markey stood there, quietly shocked, waiting for this much younger man to tell him why he had been looking for him.

"I have lived an evil life, but now I'm a Christian. I'm very sorry for the things that I did. And one of the things that I did was that I stole from you. Week after week."

The older man shuffled from one foot to the other as it was explained to him how George had lightened his pockets and wallet.

When he considered that Markey was well filled-in with the background, George got around to outlining the purpose of the search. It was this. It was simple.

"I have come looking for you to give you this money back," and with that the one-time-thief pressed into Markey Moore's gloved hand enough money to make restitution for all that had been stolen.

There was silence for a few moments. As he waited for some reaction George noticed how that the droplets of drizzle had collected on the old man's cap. And his muffler. Even on his eyebrows. Markey was nervous. Obviously embarrassed. Totally taken aback.

Since there was no immediate reaction George talked again. He told about his return to God, and about the income tax rebate. Then he stopped. It looked as though Markey had recovered sufficiently to make some sort of response.

The little old man looked straight at George and said, "I never knew anything about this. Funny that I never missed the money." He stopped for a breath, and probably to consider the whole matter, then carried on. "So you're a thief then. I could take you to the barracks you know!"

It was George's turn to feel uncomfortable. Ill at ease. Markey had stared at him and through him with those piercing little eyes.

"I know sir," he replied quietly. "And you would have every

right to do so. But my wife and child are up in the house praying about this very point. That I won't end up in court."

Markey thought again before he spoke. They had both forgotten about the drizzle and the damp as Markey asked, half-statement-half-question. "You say you're a Christian then?"

"Yes, that's right." George wondered what was coming next. "I've just been telling you the story."

"Do you know what Jesus done with the thief on the cross?" Markey had a sincere but simple grasp of the Bible, but he wasn't too hot on English grammar.

"Yes" George said. "He forgave him."

"Well, I'm a born again Christian too and I forgive you," the old man said with a faint smile.

Standing there on the footpath gazing at this kindly little Christian man, his face wrinkled with age and his clothes far-from-new, George wept. Tears mingled with the mizzle-mask on his face. He let them flow unchecked. He was so relieved. So grateful. Overcome.

As far as Markey was concerned however, the matter was over. Finished. Done with. He had to get home.

Leaving George standing deep in thought the old man moved off down the footpath. Towards home. Having taken five or six short and shuffling steps he turned round. He waved his arm in a benign gesture and shouted, as loudly as an old man can shout, "You can go and tell your wife and son to get off their knees. Their prayers are answered."

Markey trailed off into the murk.

George went home too. To tell Liz and Aaron of God's answer to their prayer. He had a lighter heart, a lighter head and a lighter pocket.

There was a sense in which his repayment to Markey Moore salved George's conscience about events in the past. But the total task was by no means complete. There was money left from the income tax rebate. And there were others to be sorted out. It had to be done.

Gerry had owned a snack bar at the top of the Avoniel

Road. George had spent some weeks of his summer holidays working for Gerry, for a few successive years.

He had sold drinks and crisps, ice cream and lollipops in a kiosk on the beach at Ballyholme. Lovely on busy sunny days. Boring on windy wet ones. And the pay wasn't great.

Looking back on those days George remembered all too vividly that his handlings of the takings hadn't been one-hundred-percent-honest. Maybe not even fifty-percent.

So he traced Gerry. The former corner-shop proprietor was now the manager of a successful East Belfast company.

George was shown into the office and there was Gerry. Same old Gerry but no soiled-shop-coat now. All dressed up in an expensive suit behind a polished desk. Covered with business-like papers, shiny pens and little flip-over calendars. Impressive.

After George had explained who he was, Gerry asked him, "Well George, what can I do for you?"

"I just want to pay you back some money—" was the opener, and then the whole story came out. How that George had diddled him years ago, how that he was now a Christian, and how that he felt he should make some kind of effort to pay people back. At least in so far as he could.

Gerry listened to the tale as it was told. It was manager-type listening. You hope that he's listening to you, but you're sure that he's thinking of half-a-dozen other things as well. George was happy enough to be given the opportunity to talk at all though.

When the account and explanation were all complete George awaited Gerry's response. He was a kind man and in a position to show it.

"I don't want that money, George," he said. "In fact I don't need it now, but I must say I appreciate what you're doing.

So you work out what to do with it. I'm sure you will think of something."

George assured him that he would, thanked him, and left.

Where do I go from here? He wondered.

He pondered it for a day or two. Talked to Liz about it a time or two, and then he remembered Hugh and Rita McVeigh, whose saintly lives had made a deep impression on his soul.

When George had been a Teddy boy, years before, a friend and he had found their daughter's handbag with money and jewellery in it. On the Castlereagh Road.

They had spent the money, kept the jewellery and dumped the handbag. When the matter had been investigated, Hugh and Rita had saved George from being prosecuted, by refusing to press charges against him. He had always been grateful to the family for that. Now he had an opportunity to express his deep regard in a practical way, he felt.

He bought a large box of groceries and took them to his former Christian neighbours, but true to form they said that the Lord had provided all that they needed, and redirected the supplies to a lady with a big family of young children in a nearby home.

Hugh and Rita became two of George's most valued friends and prayer supporters in the years that lay ahead. Hugh (who has now gone to be with his Lord) would pray for him daily with weeping that God would use George to bring souls to his precious Saviour.

And still there was money left. So he thought of others whom he had cheated in any way. Those he remembered he repaid. And still there was some money left.

The remainder he distributed. Not in cash but in coal. And groceries. Bagfuls and boxfuls. He asked some friends living in the poorer streets of East Belfast if they knew anybody in need. In straits. Real difficulties.

If George was given their names, they were given the goods. He had coal and food delivered to people who needed them.

Until eventually the income tax rebate was finished. Every last penny of it.

Liz didn't get the shopping basket out of it, because George believed that it was from God. For something else.

But if Liz didn't get the basket, George certainly got the chances. Chances to tell other people about something wonderful.

When somebody came to his door to thank him, he would say, "Don't thank me. Thank God. Let me tell you what I mean—"

When somebody told him that he was very kind he would respond with something like, "I'm not kind. Don't kid yourself. But God is very kind. Let me tell you what I mean—"

The income tax rebate had provided him with many useful contacts. Allowed him to renew many old acquaintances. Presented him with a contact-point to tell his amazing story to many wondering listeners.

And God hadn't finished with him yet.

Not by a long chalk.

CHAPTER 16
A Jordan To Cross

The Hughes Tool Factory experience that had been so vital in George's return to God, was to come to an end. Suddenly and unexpectedly, but of dire necessity. For a very down-to-earth reason.

George started to be sick. He was nauseated. But even worse than that. He was physically sick. Out loud. More and more often. Awful!

It all started with the oil. The smell of it. Oil, heavy machine oil, was an essential lubricant in an engineering works. Working in that situation day after day, George was coming to the stage where even the smell of oil on his overalls was making him want to be sick.

It took a few weeks for George and Liz to realise that perhaps the Divine Designer was at work again. One evening he prayed, quite simply, "Lord, are you allowing me to be sick so that I have to move? I will leave it in Your hands. You led me into the Hughes Tool Factory, but if You don't heal me You know that I'm going to have to leave. Please show me Your will. Amen."

In their daily study time a few evenings later George and Liz were reading about Abraham. Leaving the place where he lived -and the Bible said, "he went out not knowing where he was going." They then thought of the children of Israel going out of Egypt. Both examples of people that God was leading. Out. Out and away from a familiar environment into a strange and uncharted one.

Could this be the case for George? Get up. Get out. Get going.

They decided that perhaps this might be the answer. Were they going to be forced to give it a try? Things couldn't go on as they were for very much longer.

And they didn't. It was a Thursday morning. Belfast had roused itself and was rumbling into life. George was out of the house and walking down towards the bus stop when suddenly he had to turn back. He returned home. In a mighty hurry. Exploding through the front door, he dashed along the hall to the downstairs bathroom. To be violently sick. Yet again.

When he emerged from the bathroom the overall was off. With his mind firmly made up he walked into the living room where Liz was standing. She had heard him bursting back again and she could make a good guess at the reason why.

"Liz," he announced quite decisively. "That's it. That's the last straw. I'm not going back. I can stick it no longer."

They sat down on the settee and wept together. George didn't want to be unemployed again, but he was all through with the Hughes Tool Factory. He had liked the job and loved the people. They were all so friendly. He had even learnt to tolerate the noise. But he hated the smell of the oil. And he had no desire to spend the rest of his days feeling that he wanted to vomit.

"Lord, why are You not healing him?" Liz pleaded. "What do You want us to do?"

When their impromptu prayer time was ended and action was demanded, George said, "I know what I'm going to do, Liz. I'm going to go out and look for another job. Just like Abraham - I'm going to trust God to lead me. He went out not knowing where he was going. So will I."

That decision having been made, George changed his clothes, combed his hair a couple of times, and set off for the bus-stop again. He didn't feel sick now. Just a sort of weird. He felt that he knew where he was going and yet he didn't know where he was going. All at once. Funny peculiar.

Boarding a city-bound bus he set out to look for new employment. But where?

As the bus came towards the bottom of the Castlereagh Road, just before "John Long's Corner," George felt that he should alight. Why, he didn't know. He was just sure that he should. So he did.

Knowing that a job behind the counter in one of the variety of colourful shops that lined the road was not what he wanted, he began to walk. On impulse.

Having walked a few street-lengths he found himself standing on the Cregagh Road, looking up Ravenhill Avenue. "There's not much point in going up there," he reasoned with himself. "There are no factories or businesses up there." However his mind and his logic had no part in the matter. His feet took control of the situation.

So he walked up Ravenhill Avenue.

As he passed rows of tidy dwellings he was about to give the whole area up as a residential waste-of-time when he spotted what appeared to be a warehouse. On Ravenhill Avenue. Could this be a business premise of some sort?

There were no revolving displays or flashing lights to indicate what kind of place it was. There wasn't even a decent hand-painted hit-you-on-the-eyeball sign that George could see. But he needed to know what they did in there. Would they need just one more willing worker?

After giving the place a thorough scrutiny from a distance George moved forward to take a closer look at the only thing, which he could see that might reveal the nature of the establishment. A small notice on an outside door.

He walked up to the door and read, "SPAR. (John Henderson Ltd.,)" The names didn't mean too much to him and he was just turning to go when a car drew up. It seemed like a massive purring giant to George who had a choice of two modes of transport. Shanks's Mare or Corporation Bus.

A well-dressed, middle-aged man stepped out of the car. "Now there's a real gentleman," thought George. Long black overcoat, black hat, and black rolled umbrella. "Successful businessman," was stamped all over him.

The gentleman smiled at him and asked kindly, "Can I help you?"

Totally overawed by the man's appearance of importance George was taken unawares by his question.

"No. No-No. No thanks," he stammered. "I was just-just-just reading the notice."

The executive entered the building, and George headed for home. He felt that he had let himself down somehow. But he didn't know how.

Liz had been watching for him coming home. She could hardly wait to hear what had happened. Would somebody come running out of a shop or office or factory as George walked past and shout "Hi mister! Would you like a job in here?" No. She didn't think it would work like that.

When he did arrive home George told her about his experiences. In response to her eager questions.

She heard about where he had got off the bus. And his walkabout. About Ravenhill Avenue and the warehouse in a street of houses. Then there was the big car and the gracious gentleman. He concluded the account of his walking tour of East Belfast with the remark, "I wouldn't be a bit surprised if yon man was the boss, Liz. He certainly looked like the boss!"

That evening after tea they were reading the Scriptures together again. Daily sharing time. It was about the children of Israel. Turning back at the last minute. If they had gone directly they would have been in The Promised Land. Immediate possession. But they reneged when they saw the giants. They went out from Egypt and God was with them. But because of fear they missed their big chance. When the next generation eventually did go in they had a Jordan to cross.

Sitting by the fire, just about an hour later, George was scanning the pages of the "Belfast Telegraph". The "Situations Vacant" section was of particular interest to him.

Suddenly his eyes were riveted on to an advertisement. It seemed to jump out of the page at him.

"Liz listen to this!" He looked and spoke across to where she was sitting "SPAR. (John Henderson Ltd.) Ravenhill Avenue," he read out. Slowly. Distinctly. Like a six-year-old with a brand new reading-book. Afraid that he might miss out a word. "Wholesale warehouse order assembler required. Apply in person to above address after 10.00 a.m. on Monday morning."

"I'm going to see about that job, Liz," he continued as he released his grip on the "Belfast Telegraph", leaving it to fold itself up whatever way it liked and flutter to the floor in an untidy heap beside him.

"Just imagine, Liz," George was full of it now. "That's the very place that I was at this morning. And I'm sure that the man who spoke to me was the owner. I should have asked him if he needed any workers. But I was too scared!"

"You might have had another job by now if you hadn't been so shy, George." Liz smiled at him and taunted him gently. "You'll just have to join the queue on Monday morning now."

And join the queue on Monday morning was exactly what he did! When George arrived for interview there seemed to be dozens of people there. Some were standing. Some were sitting. Some were silent. Some were speaking.

The younger men just fresh from school or college were talking about examinations they had passed and diplomas they had done.

The older men were the ones with the working shins and the calloused hands. They were talking about previous warehouse jobs they had held.

There was one posh Englishman who talked about anything and everything to anybody who would listen.

George said nothing. He was one of the silent minority. If there was one person sitting there, he was sure there must be forty.

As he sat quietly, looking and listening, a sense of despondency gripped him. "I haven't a pup's chance in here," he thought. "If I had only spoken to the man last week. Could this be my Jordan to cross?"

"Mr. Bates, could you come this way please?" He was startled out of his reverie. Someone was calling him for an interview.

When he was shown into the office a young man rose to greet him.

"Pleased to meet you Mr. Bates," he began. Then beckoning with his hand the man continued, "Would you like to come and take a seat over here?"

George liked this young man with the dark wavy hair and rimless glasses. "Must be some kind of a foreman or supervisor," he decided to himself.

Following the opening generalities about the weather there were the normal preliminary questions. Full name? Address? Previous employment? Experience of wholesale grocery trade? The prospective employee answered every question confidently. He felt at ease with this could-be-employer. Felt somehow that he had known him all his life.

"What religious denomination do you belong to Mr. Bates?" The man-behind-the-desk was almost at the end of his list of questions.

After hesitating only momentarily George replied, "I believe that there's only one true Church. I'm a Christian. I just want to follow Christ. Simply, in a local assembly."

The interviewer appeared to be pleased with that response. He smiled and nodded. Obviously he understood, and believed that also.

"But you must go somewhere on a Sunday, do you not?" he persisted. He had to put something down on paper.

"Oh I do. I do," George said. "Of course I go to Church on Sunday."

"Does it have a denominational name?" was the next enquiry.

"Yes, it does," said George. Sheepishly.

"Well then, we will write that down," the young man said, "That's where you belong."

And he duly wrote it down.

Sitting in that office, being interviewed for a job, George felt a rumble of discomfort. A pang in his conscience. A contradiction in his creed.

He had told the man that he believed in only one true Church, and yet in his very next answer he had told him the name of a religious denomination to which he belonged.

"What is the point of saying that you believe in only one true Church if you don't do anything about it?"

That young man's question about church affiliation and the matter-of-fact acceptance of his answer had given George something to think about.

The interview was almost over. The final question gave George an opportunity to pose one of his own.

"Is there anything that you would like to ask me?" was the invitation. Some of those interviewed didn't have any further questions. George had.

Feeling that he knew this "foreman" as a friend he slid forward in his chair, leaned his elbow on a corner of the desk looked straight into his eyes and enquired, "Tell me this. Is the boss in here a Christian?"

John Agnew found it difficult to keep a straight face. In his friendly blissful ignorance George had no idea that he was talking to a junior partner in the firm. A son of the boss! Not just some charge-hand or other.

His youthful appearance belied a maturing business acumen. Smiling coyly he replied, "Well they say that he is. He may well be. Why do you ask?"

"Why do I ask?! Let me tell you why I ask. I ask because I feel that God guided me to him one day last week," George continued. He then told of his revulsion at the smell of oil, the sickness, and the need for a change of working environment, Abraham, the random bus-ride, his walk up Ravenhill Avenue...

This was certainly something different in the line of an interview. John had pushed his chair away from his desk, sat back and was listening intently.

The tale was almost told. George brought it to a climax with another question. Feeling that he must somehow identify the man-in-black, he said, "The man I saw last Thursday got out of a big car. He was wearing a long back overcoat and a black hat and was carrying a black rolled umbrella. Does that sound like the boss to you?" Pausing a moment to contemplate a final sentence with which to bring his narrative to a suitable conclusion, he finished with, "I said to my wife when I got home that I wouldn't be a bit surprised if that had been the boss that I was talking to."

"That sounds like him indeed," the young man replied, rising from his seat, conscious that there were still about two dozen applicants awaiting an interview. "It was probably our managing director that you were talking to."

With that he put out his hand. They shook hands, and just as George was turning to walk towards the door John said cheerily, "Thank you for coming Mr. Bates. You will be hearing from us in a few days time."

George thanked him and left.

Those ensuing days of waiting seemed to be unending. He couldn't go back to the Hughes Tool Factory. He had to be finished with it!

Then one morning the letter came. Would it bring welcome news? Having ripped open the envelope, George glanced at the bold letter-heading "SPAR. John Henderson Ltd." and began to read ...

9th May 1968

Dear Mr. Bates,

We are pleased to offer you the position of order assembler as from Monday, 20th May.

Please report to.........."

Without even waiting to finish the letter he called out to Liz, "I've got that job, Liz! Down in the Spar place on Ravenhill Avenue."

They were so pleased. Excited. Relieved. Thankful. God had answered their prayers again.

He had gone the long way round. But the Jordan had been crossed.

In spite of the delay.

In spite of the discouragement.

The capstan lathe setter operator was now to become a wholesale order assembler.

Another job. Free of oily-smelling-sickness.

But more than that. A new experience. And he was having plenty of them.

But more, much more, than that. A different spiritual training ground.

The Hughes Tool Factory had been George's spiritual nursery. Jim Moore had been his patient teacher. There he had taken his first teetering steps of faith.

As he began to go forward, on unsteady but strengthening spiritual legs, he needed firm but kind spiritual hands to hold as he went along. And to hold him. Sometimes steadying him, sometimes swinging him over the muddy puddles of sin. Even picking him up now and again when he had clattered down, grazing his tender spiritual knees and elbows.

He had been guided by God to Spar, to find those strong but gentle hands. Here he was to learn a lot. Here he was to see Christian love in action.

The guiding hands and gracious lives that were to shape his spiritual progress in the years to come were those of John Agnew and his father, whose identity his careful son had so cunningly concealed, Mr. William Agnew.

The gentleman with the black umbrella.

The boss!

CHAPTER 17

A Large Upstairs Room

In their newly found close communion with God -their daily delight in Divine deliverance -there was another problem for George and Liz. Something that worried them. A chilling blast from an ill spent past.

It was their old mates. Meeting their mates. Their old friends from their drinking days.

On various occasions the doorbell rang and when either of them had gone to answer it they had found one or some of their friends standing on the step. When they were invited into the house they would often produce a bottle of booze but invariably they would come off with a switcher or two.

Taking the name of the Lord their God in vain.

There was a time when that kind of behaviour would have been acceptable. Normal. Commonplace. Expected, even.

It was different now.

George took the first opportunity that he was given to let his old mates know that. Before they continued too long. And as graciously as possible. He would say something like, "Let me tell you, before you go any further -Liz and I don't curse any more. And we don't drink either. God has come into our lives. He has changed us. We are Christians now. We want to live for God."

Some of them stood there. Rooted to the spot. Dumb founded. Their eyes grew larger and their lower lips dropped lower in disbelief. When they were able to speak again, and had half-taken in what they had just been told, they used to respond with a, "Sorry we didn't know," or "We never heard that!" or even "You! A Christian!"

They would then offer some sort of excuse or apology make straight for the street, and catch the next bus into the city centre.

George and Liz always tried to persuade them that they were welcome to stay. But they never did. Things had changed in the Bates household. It wasn't the place that it used to be. They sensed it. They felt that God was there. But they didn't want to be anywhere near where God was in residence. So they cleared out. And usually didn't come back.

After one such incident George said to Liz, when their former friends had gone, "Liz, we need to install some sort of an early warning system. To prevent our friends being embarrassed. One of those pictures you can get with Bible verses on them would probably do."

Liz agreed. "That would be a good idea, George. It would let people see that we are Christians. At least it would give us a chance to explain. We must get one some day."

But where? Or what?

A few days later they were looking in the window of a Christian bookshop. Taking it all in. Discussing the books on display. Up until recently they would never have looked in such a window. Didn't interest them. Now they never passed one. They were hungry for spiritual food.

"There's just the very thing for the wall," Liz said, pointing to a picture-frame towards the back of the window. The words of the motto were an affirmation of identification. An acknowledgement of The Management. It read:

"Christ is the Head of this house. The Unseen Guest at every meal. The Silent Listener to every conversation."

"That's it Liz! You're right! That's the very thing!" George replied enthusiastically. "Come on in and we will buy it."

So in they went and bought it. Then they carried it home. The lady in the shop had been generous with her brown paper and sticky tape -but when they unwrapped it carefully they hung it above the fireplace. Plonk in the middle of the chimneybreast. Where nobody entering the room could miss it. You opened the door and there it was... demanding your attention.

And it worked a treat!

People would come in saying, "George we were wondering if you and Liz would be free to join us for a drink down in..."

Stopped dead.

Scratched their head.

Then said, "Hey, that's new." And pointed to, nodded towards, or simply stared at, the words-on-the-wall.

"Yes," one or other of their hosts would respond, "And something else is new as well. We have found a new life in Christ. As it says there, "Christ is the ... "

Same reaction. A polite and purposeful, but mostly permanent, withdrawal.

It had done the trick! Served its purpose. Set the scene. Shown "their colours". Saved embarrassment.

As with many potent remedies, however - it was to prove powerful in the present problem - but it was also to have deep-seated and far-reaching side effects.

George's sleep-pattern had been affected. He was finding it difficult to get to sleep. And if he got to sleep was finding difficulty in staying asleep. He would wake up again in the middle of the night.

It was another question of conscience that troubled him.

"Is Christ really the head of this house?" it asked. Time and time again. Night after night. "You have it hanging up on the wall of your living room for everybody to see. If it is true - and Christ is the head of this house - why are you sleeping in the biggest and best bedroom?"

There developed a conflict. His human reason told him he was daft. His Christian conscience told him he was a charlatan.

So he couldn't sleep. He lay tossing and turning. Every night. Thinking. Reasoning. Often praying.

One night Liz could bear it no longer. With her restless husband churning about in the bed beside her it hadn't been long until her sleep pattern had been affected as well!

She sat upright beside him, and exclaimed as she tried to repossess a few blankets, "That's it! I've had enough of this! There's something wrong with you George. What on earth is it? Why can you not lie at peace?" She sounded exasperated.

He pretended he hadn't heard her at first. Didn't answer.

"Come on, George, what is it?" Liz wasn't going to give up that easily. She knew that he was awake.

And he knew that he had to answer. He was caught. Cornered. He must be honest, too. His lying days were long-since gone.

"I'm almost ashamed to tell you what's bothering me, Liz," he began sheepishly. "It's so absurd. It doesn't even make sense."

"Whatever it is, I want to hear it anyway. Out with it George." Liz was mystified now.

Then he explained to her what was troubling him. "Who is the head of this house?" was what it all amounted to. He thought that she would begin to laugh at something so ludicrous. He thought that she would decide that he was losing his reason. Away with the birds.

But no!

She didn't laugh. She understood George and his God-centred conscience. And besides, it was the middle of the night and she needed some sleep!

His longsuffering wife had a very practical solution to the problem. Slipping out of the bed she grabbed all the bedclothes in one untidy straggling heap in her arms and then marched blankets trailing, into the smaller back bedroom. George got out of the bed as well. There wasn't much else he could do since the covers were gone! He stood mesmerised for a moment.

When Liz returned for the pillows she just remarked, almost casually, "So that's what it's all been about then. Are you not coming, George?" He followed her into the other room where she had already started to make up the spare bed.

It didn't take long to prepare, and soon they were getting back into bed. In a smaller bedroom. Having vacated the large one.

And George slept like a log! Out like a light! He began to sleep better than he had done for days. For weeks!

Meanwhile, as their sleep patterns improved, the appearance of their former bedroom deteriorated. The room that had been set aside to allow Christ to assume the position of "Head of the house" in every way possible, had fast become a junk room. A-shove-it-in-there-until-it-gets-to-the-attic room. It contained an old cot, a pram, a small variety of suitcases, a bigger variety of empty cardboard boxes, unused Christmas presents, faded framed photographs. And much more. Some high-class-clutter. Some useless odds and ends.

A box-room. A storeroom

The Lord's room?

George had watched with mild dismay as it had filled with all kinds of discards. Surely if his experience had been of God it must be destined for something more than that!

So he prayed. As he prayed about it, and continued to ask God for His will as to its use, he felt a strong affinity with the man in the Bible. The man who had a large upstairs room - furnished. Jesus had asked His disciples to prepare it. Get everything ready. For His use.

That's what it could be used for. Slowly the vision emerged in George's mind. A room in a house in a street where people could come and talk about God. And to Him. Not a church. Some of the guys and girls that George and Liz knew were drug addicts. Dropouts. They wouldn't want to go to church. No. A large upstairs room. That could be the place.

He could prepare the room. A place where the Lord could meet with people. And people could be introduced to Him.

It could be prepared for Him.

Exclusively His.

The Lord's room.

In the firm belief that the room should be prepared as a Divine retreat, Liz and he began to plan carefully and prayerfully.

What would be needed? It would have to be redecorated for a start. Obviously. Then they would need a new carpet. Curtains. Chairs. A change of light shade.

It was fine to have plans. No harm in that. But plans on paper, or dreams in your head, translated into furniture and fittings in a large upstairs room all cost money. Of which they didn't have a lot.

They were talking about it after teatime one evening. George was standing in the living room talking through to Liz who was working in the kitchen. Revising their plans. For the umpteenth time.

"Liz, have you any idea how much all this will cost?" he asked, concerned.

Coming out of the kitchen, drying-cloth-clutching-half-dried-cup in her hand, Liz advanced a couple of steps into the living room. She was deep in thought. Costing. Calculating. Then she spoke. "It will all cost about one hundred pounds," she reckoned.

A hundred pounds! George hadn't thought it would cost that much! At a time when the average wage for a working person was fifteen pounds a week!

"I have lost my reason this time," he decided to himself. "Flipped my lid sure enough."

Later that evening the plans for the preparation of the room upstairs were uppermost in both their minds. "We should pray about it Liz," George suggested.

So they did.

"Lord we were so convinced that You were guiding us about this," he began. "But if it's going to take as much as a hundred pounds then You know that we haven't got that amount of money. Lord show us Your will. Please guide us we pray..."

When they had finished their prayer time they agreed that

they wouldn't mention their upstairs-room-project or its financial restraints to anyone. Only God.

So they didn't tell anyone. Only God.

Three days later George and Liz were visiting in East Belfast. As the evening wore on, supper was over and time-to-go-time drew near. Suddenly the man of the house stood up. It was unexpected.

Reaching what appeared to be a roll of notes to George he said firmly, "I believe I have to give you that."

George was staggered. Nobody had ever so openly offered him money before. And besides that, since having had an experience of living contact with a gracious God, he and Liz had discarded many of the trappings of their former life, seeking to live clearly and plainly for the God who had changed their lives in so many ways. Their simple motto had been, "Silver and gold have I none."

"I can't take that," George retorted immediately. "I have never taken money from anybody without working for it, and I won't be starting now."

His host kept his cool. He merely continued calmly. "You can say what you like and protest as much as you like, but all I know is that I have to give it to you."

His placid persistence only made George worse at first. He was going to argue it out with the man. He was almost ready to fight with him.

"I don't want it and I won't be taking it!" was his deliberate protest.

"Whether you want it or not doesn't matter, you will be taking it!" the benefactor went on. Unruffled.

Something about his attitude changed George's. Somehow he knew that he wasn't going to win this argument. He had to take the money.

Partly to placate his pride, and partly to permit him to accept the preferred gift, George mellowed his tone. And changed his tack.

"Well I suppose if it was used for the Lord's work it

would be O.K." he responded quite mildly. He was seeing a compromise. A way out.

"Use it for whatever you want," his friend replied. "All I know is that I have to give it to you."

George took the money. Under duress.

Something deep inside him told him that he shouldn't - but then something even deeper inside him told him that he should.

So he did.

A short time after, as they were standing at the bus stop on the lower end of the Castlereagh Road waiting for the bus that would take them home, George remembered the money. They were alone at the bus-stop, the pair of them, so George decided to count it. Out of curiosity. He had no idea what he was going to do with it. None at all.

He huddled forward and started to count. Flicking the edges of the notes through his fingers. When he had finished he started to weep. Just burst out crying. Big tears ran down his cheeks. As he was wiping them away with a handkerchief, hastily pulled from another pocket, Liz noticed.

"What's wrong George? What's the matter?" she enquired. She was startled. So sudden, these tears.

"Liz, there's one hundred pounds here! Exactly one hundred pounds," her husband answered. He was excited. Humbled. Overcome with joy. He remembered the room. For the Lord. And their estimated cost of refurbishing.

One hundred pounds.

As Liz and he stood there, guarding that lonely bus-stop sign on a mild, pleasant late Spring evening, George felt slightly foolish. A grown man standing weeping. Intermittent traffic grumbled past. A group of passing youths called out to each other across the street. He hoped they hadn't seen him. He was almost sure they hadn't.

When the bus came and they stepped lightly aboard, they had learnt another lesson about the goodness and kindness of their bountiful God. It was a basic lesson. It was simply this - When the Lord sends you out to bake a cake. He supplies the ingredients!

They were to prove the truth of that repeatedly in the days that were yet to come!

CHAPTER 18
Furnished

George and Liz had a job to do now. A task to perform. A room to furnish. God had provided the wherewithal. It had to be used prudently. Prayerfully. For Him. The walls were all painted white except one. The remaining wall was covered with wood-finish panel board. The ceiling they covered with polystyrene tiles. Warm and bright. A circular fluorescent light was fitted in the centre of the ceiling.

With the decoration complete, a carpet and curtains had to be chosen. After looking in a few different shops and comparing a variety of prices, they made their choice. It was for blue. Royal blue. Dark and rich. For carpet and curtains.

They arranged for the carpet to be fitted and the curtains to be made. Then they painstakingly hung them up. Full length, ceiling to floor, crushed velvet.

The room was beginning to take on a new look. But what about furniture? As they had been decorating the walls and ceiling, and covering the windows and floors, they had been discussing the furniture. What kind of chairs would they need? And how many?

Passing a furniture shop on the corner of Templemore Avenue, late one evening, George spied in the centre of the well-lit front window exactly what he wanted for the upstairs room.

It was a folding chair. Square wooden seat. Wooden back and it folded flat. Easily transported, stacked or stored. The kind you could nip your fingers in if you were not careful. Snapped shut - like a mousetrap - if pushed too hard. A number of them would be the very thing. Suitable and serviceable in a room set aside for prayer.

His heart skipped a beat. Pity it's so late! He would have loved to discuss the chairs with someone right away.

It was then that he noticed that although the shop appeared to be all closed up, the front door was lying very slightly ajar. George gave it a gentle push. It opened. He gazed inquisitively inside.

As he scanned the interior he noticed a young man in the dim distance of the depths of the shop. Right away at the back of the premises. In what seemed like a workshop. Quietly and industriously staining and polishing a table. All alone.

Who was this? Working at twenty-five-to-eleven at night? And just a youth. Couldn't be more than sixteen or seventeen.

"Excuse me please," George called out. "Could I speak to you a moment?"

He had expected an abrupt response, but was pleasantly surprised when the young man looked up and smiled.
Leaving his work the teenager walked briskly towards the front door.

George stepped inside to meet him.

"Hello! What can I do for you?" he called out cheerily as he approached.

Apologetically George began, "I know you are closed, and I can see that you're busy. But I'm very interested in those folding chairs."

It wasn't long until a genial and patient young man, Victor, had heard the story of the upstairs room. To date partly-furnished.

George expected the youth to express some surprise at such an offbeat story. But he didn't. Just stood grinning and nodding his head. It was George that was surprised to a certain degree. Only a Christian could swallow this uncanny story first go, he reasoned. So he enquired, "If you don't mind me asking, are you a Christian?"

After further conversation George learned that this amiable youth was one of a large family from Newtownards.

So poor that they occasionally had to eat berries from the trees. To suppress the pangs of hunger. Augment their plain and wholesome, but often meagre, diet. Now, although he was just a teenager, yet because he was reckoned to be old enough to stand on his own two feet, the family had asked him to leave home. Try and find a job for himself. And somewhere else to live.

He appreciated the sense of the situation. He saw the fix his parents were in. So he procured a tiny flat in Templemore Avenue above a shop. And he had found himself a job, in the furniture shop. Working from early morning until late at night. For buttons.

George's heart went out to him.

When the shop had been locked up, a short time later, he accompanied Victor round to his little flat. After a cup of tea and a chat about God's marvellous dealings in his life, George had the joy of leading him to faith in Christ.

As he was leaving the flat in the early hours of the morning, Victor said to him, "By the way, don't worry about those chairs. I'll get you as many of them as you want. And I'll see if the boss would give you a pound or two off them."

George was pleased as he walked homewards because God had led him to a needy young man. And had furnished the Lord's room with chairs for good measure!

When he arrived home he poured out his heart in praise to God. For His goodness.

And in prayer to God. For Victor. That He would prosper this kindly young man, now a child of His, in the furniture business. Take this Oliver Twist who was working so willingly in the backroom of a furniture shop. Bring him out into the front window of the furniture world.

Victor was as good as his word. He spoke to the boss. George got his chairs. At a reduced price. Eighteen of them. A dozen-and-a-half, for the upstairs room.

And God was as good as His word. Victor came to the very forefront of the furniture business in Northern Ireland in later years.

With chairs to sit on now, and a carpet to kneel on, all they needed was a source of heat. For that they bought an oil-filled radiator. It would be cold should they stay late or pray late on a winter night.

The room was finally fully furnished. Ready for the Lord to meet his followers. Smelling of new paint, fresh fabric and real wood.

Clean and bright. Refreshingly renewed.

Ready for action.

Prepared for Him.

Throughout the whole refurbishment programme they had kept close tabs on their expenditure. They knew they must. God had provided them with the money. They couldn't be wasteful.

When the last bill had been settled they did their sums. Balanced the books. Counted up their every expense.

They had a large upstairs room.

Furnished.

Total cost. One hundred pounds!

CHAPTER 19
Open Secrets

Now that the room was complete, how was it going to be used? George and Liz were pleased with it. Almost proud of it. But it couldn't remain empty. Unused. Idle.

It was for God and had to be put into operation.

George had a burden for prayer. Secret sustained prayer. He knew God's promise. Whatever was done in secret would be rewarded openly. And open rewards would be welcome. Necessary. Vital.

On a Saturday evening visit to the always packed and Divinely-blessed Coalmen's Mission, George had this confirmed to him.

Mightily. Miraculously.

God inspired a young minister called Tommy Shaw to change the message, which he had prepared for that evening.

As the crowds were cramming in, he was sitting on the platform, head bowed. Having an encounter with God. It was plain for all to see. He was in anguish of mind. Struggling in soul.

When the time came for him to speak he stood up. And read from the Bible in John chapter three. About Nicodemus. About being born again. That's what he had come to talk about.

Then he confessed to the congregation that since coming into the Hall he was being powerfully and irresistibly persuaded to change his message.

To speak about prayer. He admitted that he had never addressed a public gathering on that subject before.

But he knew that he daren't disobey such a compelling conviction.

So he changed his message. And spoke about prayer. Without any prior preparation.

People were gripped by a sense of God. The awe of an Unseen Presence.

Revival exploded in their hearts.

George left that meeting in another world. The third heaven. He walked all the way home. On air. It hadn't even occurred to him that he had forgotten to take the bus!

That experience had been his affirmation.

Prayer for revival would not only be important.

It could prove to be critical.

The state of affairs in Belfast was worrying. The city had been rocked by the impact of the now-started and rapidly escalating troubles. Shooting and bombing were becoming deadly daily deeds. People were losing their limbs or their lives. And many of them didn't know God. Some of them had despised God. Deliberately rejected Him.

George felt for them. He knew where they were. He had been there too.

There was a glaring need for revival in Northern Ireland.

There was a desperate need for prayer.

George prayed alone about who should pray along with him. Then he thoughtfully compiled a list. A list of nine. Seven people plus Liz and himself. He felt that these nine people should meet regularly and pray. Fervently and earnestly. Seriously and systematically.

In the upstairs room.

Then God would bless.

He had promised that He would.

There were the Stitts. Lily and Davy. Prayer warriors with a simple faith. There was young Victor. And Jim Moore. Spiritual giant. There was Hughie Sloan. And there were others.

George undertook to contact the seven people personally. To explain his conviction. Invite their co-operation.

In the days that followed he finally succeeded in contacting all of them. It had meant late nights and long walks. But he felt that God had wanted him to do it. So he did it. Happily.

Most of them agreed to come and pray. Some perhaps with slight reservations. George-is-so-keen-it-would-be-ashame-to-disappoint-him attitude. It'll do no harm just to go for a night or two. Please him no end. Would be a pity to let him down.

A date and time were arranged for the initial gathering. To put the-room-set-aside to its proper use.

Contacting God.

Five of them turned up and they began by listening to a tape-recording by Stephen Olford. About revival. Then with George and Liz they prayed. No time limit was set on these precious prayer power stations.

The prayer sessions progressed as planned. Into the room, onto their knees, and straight into the presence of God. There could be no mistaking it. They all knew that God was going to work.

They prayed seriously and systematically. Earnestly and fervently. Like Jacob in the Bible, they were in effect saying to God, by the depth of their conviction and reality of their contact, "We're not going to let You go unless You bless us!"

Their prayer was for revival. For a mighty movement of God.

God heard.

God answered.

The God who had heard in secret was making His Own preparations. To reward them openly.

In addition to their overall concern for revival in Ireland and a wonderful working of God in their country, George and Liz had a personal plea. It was simple. It was this.

"Lord bring people. Young people. Any young people. No matter who they are or where they come from. Bring young people to this house. To this room. So that we can teach them about You."

It was a sincere request. And God heard it. And granted it.

He brought them.

The links that God used were two enthusiastic young Christians. Raymond and Robert. These men were contacting drug-addicts in city-centre Belfast almost every day.

But these addicts needed a quiet place to talk. To someone who cared. About themselves. About their scene. About God.

That place was to be the Lord's room.

Paul came. Jimmy Hendrix haircut. One big blob of ginger hair that flopped about. His mind fuddled by drugs.

Terry came. All flower power and blowing bubbles. Gaily coloured shapeless clothes. "Peace, man" to everybody he met.

Others came. Some of them up to their necks in witchcraft. Practising the occult.

All of them on drugs. A motley crew.

As these young people came up to visit George and Liz the neighbours in Glenview Park looked on in amazement. Men stopped mowing their lawns and women paused from cleaning their windows.

To watch the weirdos walk by. Up to Bates' house.

They had always known that George Bates was a "kind of an eccentric guy," but they thought that he had freaked out altogether now. Totally and entirely.

Imagine encouraging this kind of "riff-raff up into their neighbourhood! But that was exactly what the prayer-times had been all about! George and Liz had wanted to see people like that coming up to their house.

So that they could be told about God.

And His love. And His grace. And His kindness.

So that they could learn about His mighty salvation which could change powerless pointless lives. Make them useful for Him.

Many young people came. And trusted Christ. They brought others. Who trusted Christ.

So it continued. In one month alone forty young people had been brought to the Saviour. Through the influence of their former fellow-addicts.

God was answering prayer. Beyond the wildest expectations of the prevailing-prayer-team.

Numbers increased. Soon there were a score or so of them gathered every Friday night to pray. And they didn't stop to go home. They just read the Bible, prayed to God, and praised Him for His goodness. All night.

Often Liz had to make eighteen or twenty breakfasts. On a Saturday morning.

George had learnt a lot about the power of God in his life, before the "Lord's room" experience. But there was much more to learn about His power to answer prayer. He learnt through the child-like faith of a young believer. Asking God for the patently impossible.

Paul was praying. Crying to God for a child-hood friend.

"Lord You know about Fitzy," he was saying. "You know that he has left home and is living in London. You know that he has taken a vow and has had all his hair shaved off. He's in that heathen temple and there's no way the priests will ever let him get out..."

George was down on the floor beside the young man. He felt that he ought to offer to God some sort of an excuse for this fresh new Christian with the naive request. Explain things a bit.

"Ach, don't pay any attention to him. Lord," he said inwardly. "He's only a wee young convert. It's only wee Paul, Lord. He doesn't understand..."

Meanwhile Paul was continuing. In all his simplicity. Interceding with God on behalf of his friend. Whom he hadn't seen for some time.

"Lord, if he can't get out send somebody in. Send somebody in to preach the Gospel. Save him Lord! Let him get saved. And baptised..." And so he prayed on. Expecting God to answer...

And George continued. Silently apologetic. "Bless him, Lord, bless him. He means well. But You understand..."

On the next Friday night Paul came up to the house. He was bursting with joy. Producing a letter he said to George, "Here, have a read at this."

It was from London. From Fitzy.

It began:

"Dear Paul,

You will be pleased to hear that a young Brethren man came into the temple where I was. He sent the priests wild by preaching the Gospel. I got saved and I'm getting baptised next week..."

An Almighty answer to a simple prayer. A gentle rebuke to a faithless follower...

There were marvellous answers to many prayers that went up to God from that upstairs room.

George and Liz felt pleased to be part of it.

Tools to be used by the Master Carpenter. Clay to be used by the Master Potter.

They had followed His request.

Provided at His behest.

A large upstairs room. Furnished.

Could this be their life's work for God?

CHAPTER 20
Sell All That You Have

Those were marvellous days of mini-revival.

These recent contacts didn't have regular jobs as a result of their dropout lifestyle. They had all the time in the world. To walk. And talk. And sing. And generally enjoy life as it found them.

Those were the flower-power days.

The-no-need-to-worry-man,

Just-love-your-neighbour-man,

Everything-will-be-all-right-man, days.

And the Beatles were singing,

"All you need is love."

These young people had been inclined to agree. Easy enough on sunny summer afternoons.

When the daylight hours began to get shorter, and the windy-leaf-blown days of Autumn were succeeded by the biting chill of Winter nights, and the crowds in London and Belfast went home, the young people left behind on the cold wet streets began to realise that they had additional needs. Love in itself wasn't all they required.

What about shoes? And shelter?

Enough to eat? Something warm to wear?

And they didn't even have the bus fare home.

Destitute Bongo drummers.

Starving guitar strummers.

With a craving for L.S.D. and cannabis and dope of all kinds.

They needed God's love, and a lot of help and counselling.

And they came to George. They had lots to talk about and time was no object.

They could talk all night and sleep all day if they fancied.

For George it was different. He was sitting up until three or four o'clock in the morning counselling these yearning young minds. Then snatching a few hours sleep before rising at seven o'clock to go to his work.

Not only were these people searching for soul satisfaction. They were also penniless and hungry. Starving for something to eat. The only food in the house was what Liz could buy on George's wages. And no matter who came or how many came, Liz offered them some food. Physical sustenance.

She was often in tears as she prepared their own supply of food for perhaps a dozen others. But everyone always had something to eat. And there was enough left to feed George and Liz and little Aaron at breakfast time.

God made ample provision. For all. Always.

As things developed there were special meetings now on Wednesday evenings and Sunday mornings. In addition to the Friday evening prayer-time marathons. All in the Lord's room.

Babes in Christ were being weaned. Away from drugs. And on to more nourishing spiritual provision.

One day a lorry driver in Spar, George McKeown, asked the working-by-day and counselling-by-night George a question. He was a Christian, and interested.

"Tell me this, do you see all these drug addicts you talk about. Who teaches them? Into the early hours of the morning? Is it you or somebody else?"

"I do. I teach them," was the quiet response. The tone of his answer was a queer blend of humility, apology and weariness.

"But sure you have only been walking with the Lord for a couple of years. How can you teach them?" The driver was dubious.

"That's the problem," was the sincere but still immature, Bible-teacher's reply. "I'm doing the best I can. To dig into

This Is For Real

God's word and teach them. But to be honest with you I would love a bit of teaching myself."

"I thought you would," replied George McKeown. "And I believe I have the answer for you."

"What's that?" the other George enquired, curious. Hopeful.

The solution was simple. Tapes. "I'm involved in my spare time in a tape ministry," was the explanation. "I leave a tape recorder at certain houses and people gather in to hear about the Bible. We also supply the tapes."

George was intrigued. This was a new slant on things. "Who does the teaching on these tapes you're talking about?" he asked.

"Have you ever heard of Willie Mullan? From Lurgan?" was the next question.

"No I haven't," George said. He realised by the expectant tenor of the travelling tapeman's enquiry that he probably should have, but he hadn't. It sounded as though everybody in the whole wide world had heard of this Willie Mullan and he was one of the few who hadn't!

"I haven't the time to get out to hear anybody," he continued. "My house is always bunged with people."

"Well I think he's the man for your particular situation. If I bring the tape-recorder up to your house some night. Say a Wednesday? - Would you get the young folk in to listen? Then they can get the teaching. And so can you!"

"That sound's great!" was George's instant reaction. The idea appealed to him. Teaching others and being taught all at once. "When can we start?"

"As soon as you like!" was the assuring reply.

Thus began the tape-ministry teaching-time in the Lord's room. On a Wednesday evening.

The room was always well filled. And the audience were keen to learn. And share. And discuss the Bible with one another. When the humming tape had buzzed to a clicking stop.

There was something new on Sundays too. A table. A simple table for a simple ceremony.

152

These new converts wanted to remember the Lord as they felt the Bible was teaching them to do.

And they did. Every Sunday morning. Simply, sincerely and reverently.

George soon became skilled in cutting off the shoulder length hair of some of these young men. Rich in faith but couldn't afford a haircut. Hadn't been in a barber's shop for years. Now they wanted to look more normal. Discard one of the symbols of their former lifestyle.

To lead the way, George had relinquished his own teddy-boy style. Had his hair cut almost to the roots. A Christian skinhead. Saved him precious time. He didn't have to stand for ages in front of a mirror now!

As these enthusiastic young believers learnt more about the Bible, and its teachings, they wanted to obey God. In every possible way. Many of them wanted to be baptised.

So George, who was their provider of shelter, their breadwinner and barber, also arranged to have them baptised. By immersion. In the sea, around the County Down coast. Ballywalter. Sandycove. Anywhere with easy access to waist-deep water.

Public baptism for a public witness.

A public witness to a personal faith.

Liz was by now expecting their second child. And her house was busy. Always people coming and going. More like a bus-shelter on a wet day than a cosy little sit-by-the-fireside home. Yet she never complained. The Lord's room was for the Lord. And His work. And His use.

His work was being done.

His room was being used. And she was happy.

She just went to bed earlier, ignoring the voices often raised to almost shouting in effectual fervent prayer. And left them to it. Slept soundly.

George now became aware in his personal devotions that the story in the Bible about Christ's conversation with the rich young Jewish leader kept cropping up. Over and over again.

In response to the ruler's question about obtaining eternal life, part of Jesus' answer had been to exhort him to "sell all that you have, and come and follow Me."

The recurrence of these words in his mind became an obsession. George was thinking of them all the time.

When he awoke in the morning.

"Sell all..."

Before he went to sleep at night.

"Sell all that you have, and...."

And all through the day as well. At work. At home.

"Sell all that you have, and come and follow Me."

George couldn't understand it. The Lord's room was being really blessed.

People - all kinds of people - were still coming. Seeking guidance. Seeking peace. Seeking God. And he was being run off his feet. Counselling converts.

Now this.

"Sell all that you have..."

There must be some mistake. A mix-up. Crossed lines.

He had got it wrong this time for sure.

In frustration one night he prayed about it. As he had done about so many things so often before.

"Lord, if this is the Devil and he's mad at the souls who are being saved in our house, he must be a fool if he thinks this will stop us," he began.

"But Lord You know all about this verse that keeps plaguing me. If it is You, then there's no way I can talk to Liz about it. She has enough on her plate."

The prayer continued by shifting the responsibility on to God. Asking Him for some kind of sign.

"How can two walk together unless they are agreed? It would be up to you Lord to talk to her about it also. If she brings it up then I'll know that You are at work.

Please show me Your way and Your will. Amen."

With that he left it. Off his own shoulders and conscience. The onus was now on God. Let Him sort it out.

George didn't expect to hear any more about it. Had

it just been another crazy whim? Another daft notion?

Every Sunday morning was a tonic to George and Liz. George prepared the room. Specially. Carefully. Almost reverently.

Chairs around the walls. Long low table in the middle. Grape juice in a glass. Unleavened bread on a plain-white plate. Both covered with a white dust cover. Starched and spotless.

It was thrilling to see these one-time drug addicts coming up to the house. All spruced up. Faces aglow. Hearts afire.

To remember the Lord.

On one such sacred Sunday morning a young man rose to speak about the early Christian church. Selling all that they had. Having all things in common. For the Lord's sake.

Liz nudged George while the man was talking. A big dunt with her elbow. George was taken by surprise. This was so uncharacteristic. Liz usually sat listening intently to whoever was speaking.

Assuming that she must be feeling unwell, he glanced across to see what was the matter.

She looked O.K. But she was pointing to a verse in the Bible, which was lying open on her knee.

That afternoon, when everyone else had left, George asked her over dinner, "Why did you nudge me this morning, Liz? In the meeting I mean."

"It's just that verse I was pointing to. It keeps coming up time after time in my reading. About selling everything for the Lord."

The goose pimples rose on George's body. He shivered.

Slowly and deliberately he replaced the knife and then the fork on either side of the plate. Beside his almost-finished dinner. Then he pushed the plate forward towards the centre of the table.

Liz looked concerned. She wondered what had happened to him. What was coming next?

"I've got to talk to you about this, love." he said at length.

Then he told her about his verse - and its repetition. Leading to his frustration. And his prayer.

"Lord, if it's from You, make Liz mention it first."

George finished the account of his preoccupation with that verse with a resigned, "And there you are Liz. You have just done what I asked God that you would do. If it was from Him."

He folded his arms on the edge of the table. Where his dinner should have been. And stared into space. Entranced.

Liz pondered his story for a moment or two. And then reflected on her own recent experience. With the same idea.

"What does all this mean George?" she queried, quietly.

"That's what I have been trying to figure out, love," was her husband's studied response. I have been giving it a lot of thought and the only conclusion that I can come to is that God has somewhere else for us. There's no doubt that this house is too small for the work that we're doing now. Maybe God wants us to expand the work. Maybe He has a big white elephant of a house somewhere that nobody can sell. But it's got our name on it. It might need fixed up. We could all pitch in. Work at it. Then we would have a better place. Bigger. More scope to reach more people."

Ideas were beginning to form in the reservoir of his mind. They were swirling about and cascading out. In torrents of words.

He was in overdrive now. Whizzing along.

In a momentary pause he glanced over at Liz. Her attention was riveted on him. But he checked himself suddenly. Abruptly. Crashed right down through the gears. Until he was crawling along in second.

He had forgotten about something. About something that should have been so important! Liz. And her condition. She was due to have a baby in a week or two's time and here he was talking about selling out! Flitting!

"Obviously this is the wrong time to be talking like that,"

he continued. His tone was more restrained. "What with you pregnant and all."

"Never mind about that George. Or me," was the instant response from Liz. "If it's what God wants for us, I'm prepared to do it."

About a fortnight after that Sunday lunchtime conversation on Divine direction for their lives, Liz went into hospital. To have their second child.

And baby Daniel was born. Arrived howling on planet Earth. 13th May, 1970.

They were extremely happy. There were four of them now. But for George this happiness had one temporary limitation. A minor irritation. Like being slightly burnt in pursuit of a lasting deep-brown suntan.

He had to fend for himself at home.

Something else was regrettable. But unavoidable.

George had to go and visit Liz and baby Daniel in hospital. That was the pleasant bit. So he had no choice but to lock up. What they had said would be an ever open door. That was the unfortunate bit.

As he travelled on the bus to see her he wondered to himself, "What will happen when somebody comes up to the house tonight? What will they do? They know where I am. They'll probably wait until I get back!" Even though it was not a regular meeting night they had come to expect the shelter-seeking comfort-craving Bible-searchers to call. Every night.

To pray and praise.

To sit for hours. Discussing and debating. Learning about God. About real life. About heavenly love.

"Well it's in God's hands. There's nothing I can do about it tonight," he reasoned. Sensibly.

But he needn't have worried. On his arrival home, two hours later, he discovered that a packed-house meeting was going on without him. Normal service had been continued. The Lord's room was full. And so was the kitchen. And he hadn't even been in!

"I did lock the house, didn't I? Before I left. Yes I did." He had conducted a hasty self-interrogation as he had walked down the path. And heard the voices from the house.

When he opened the front door, Paul met him in the hall.

"George you forgot to leave us a key," he remarked. Pretending to be disappointed. A twinkle in his eye.

"Well how did you all get in?" George asked, bewildered. "It doesn't seem to have made a lot of difference!"

"Oh somebody just climbed up the spout and then we let ourselves in." Easy when you know how! "You left a wee window open for us!" he said.

It wasn't so easy when morning came. Liz wasn't there to help George get out to work. He had to go through their well-practised routine. On his own.

Make his own breakfast. Prepare his own "Piece."

Big change.

So he rose a little earlier. Give himself time to get everything done and have a glance at a book of devotional readings.

Between watching his toast, and making his lunch, he opened it. Anywhere. At random. Just to grab some spiritual sustenance to add to his no-frills breakfast. To help him through the day.

"Sell all that you have and come follow me."

There it was again. Popping off the page. To George's dismay. Was he not mixed up enough?

He immediately closed the book and went over to the tape-recorder in the corner of the room. There was an unmarked new tape sitting beside it. With all the coming-and-going of recent days he hadn't had a chance to hear it. He would listen to that. Instead of reading.

There was just one thought in his mind as he threaded the tape into the spool and switched on the machine. -"At all costs I must obliterate that haunting thought from my mind. Or it will dominate my thoughts for the entire day. I have plenty to think about at the minute. Without having to worry about all that again."

Screwing up the volume so that he could hear it from

whatever part of the house he happened to be rushing to, he returned to the bench. For another bite or two of his soggy, now cold and stuck-to-the-plate-with-the-damp toast.

The voice of Billy Graham thundered out from the machine, "And the Saviour said to the young man, "Sell all that you have. And come follow Me!"

This was incredulous.

George just threw himself down on his knees.

"Lord that's it!" he conceded. "The very tape-recorder is crying out to me. This can only be God.

I submit.

Where do we go from here?"

CHAPTER 21
Put Up The Sails

Hughie Sloan lived on the Old Holywood Road. Late one beautiful Saturday evening in June, George set out on the bus from the city centre to visit him.

He was sitting on the top deck of the bus. Front seat. Best spot for a good view. It would be a longish journey. There was only another couple on the upper deck.

As the bus approached the lower end of the Newtownards Road, George noticed people hiding behind gable walls and peeping out of doorways. They were all looking anxiously up the road. Everybody appeared to be terror-stricken. Scared stiff.

He was soon to understand the reason for their panicky behaviour.

A frenzied mob was surging down the road. A moving multitude. Closing on the bus.

They were looting shops. Burning cars.

In seconds they were round the bus. Like wasps round drinks-tins in litterbins.

They pushed the bus from one side - then the other. Slowly but surely they rocked it. As it rocked it gathered momentum.

Would they turn it over or burn it out with him on it?

Fearfully George looked round to see what the couple behind him were doing. They weren't there. They had vanished. Kneeling down at the front seat he prayed in a panic.

"Lord, get this bus moving!" he yelled. He hadn't intended to scream at God. But his life was in danger.

He remained on his knees at the front seat. Clutching it tightly.

Inch by inch his prayer was answered.

Gradually the bus began to move. The driver revved up the engine to full throttle. And moved three inches. Did the same again. And moved six. Same again. A foot this time.

Eventually the bus was clear of the mob. Leaving them to advance towards the city centre.

George was weak. Drained. Exhausted.

He was convinced that he should keep his head below the level of the bus window for some reason. Stay on his knees.

The next day he was to understand why. Six people had been shot on the Newtownards Road that evening. His bus had been the last illuminated moving vehicle that had passed safely through the mob and up the road.

The bus went a long way before it ever stopped. When it did, George got off. Leaving Hughie Sloan for another night, he walked home. A circuitous route. Avoiding possible flash points.

As he walked he was pouring out his grateful heart to his preserving God.

"Thank you! Thank you! Thank you, God! "He cried. Over and over again.

His heart was thumping.

His legs were shaking.

He was overcome by a tremendous sense of relief and amazement, that God was able to deliver him from such a situation. The very jaws of Death.

Stopping below an old-fashioned lamppost on the King's Road he slipped his little Bible from his pocket and opened it at random. Leaning against the lamppost for stability he looked down at his open Bible.

He read the first verse his eyes fixed upon.

It read, "Our God whom we serve is able to deliver us from the burning fiery furnace."

God seemed to be implying, "You haven't seen anything

yet George. I can do greater things for you than you can ever imagine.

Just trust Me. That's all."

Trusting is easy when you have a fair idea of the way ahead. That everything will work out for the best in the end. Somehow. Sometime.

But stepping out into the totally illogical unknown can be a different matter.

As George and Liz were to discover.

George was convinced in his own mind that it must be God's will for them to sell their house.

But when? And how would they advertise it? Who would buy it anyway? If they did sell it where would they live?

They had two young sons now. Demanding time and attention. A caring home. They couldn't just pick Aaron and Daniel up in the crook of an arm and step out onto the street!

What would happen if they put their house up for sale and the prospective buyer expected immediate possession. What would they do?

All these thoughts tormented him. The only logical solution that George could think of was that God was going to come up with His Own special offer. A bigger place at a bargain price. Somehow he would just magic it for them. If they waited.

So they waited. For something to happen.

For days. Then weeks. Then months.

Summer had turned to autumn. Green had turned to gold.

Sunny skies had given way to morning mists.

And nothing had happened.

Instead of decreasing with the passing of time, the conviction that they were to sell deepened. Increased a hundredfold.

Frustration of soul grew with it. They were perfectly persuaded in their minds what they should do. What God wanted them to do.

But they weren't doing it.

Now they were afraid of holding back on God. They had never done so before, and they didn't want to be guilty of it now.

Whenever they had the chance to chat to each other, in their less busy baby-minding-nappy-changing-bottle-making moments, their conversation would gravitate to the same subject. Into the same orbit. Debating their dilemma.

To sell or not to sell?

To obey in faith or ignore through fear?

Not only was it the most common topic of their conversations. It had become the predominant theme of their prayers.

What were they going to do?

One evening when the children were asleep and the house was unusually quiet, George and Liz were sitting by the fire. It was pleasing to snatch a few moments of peace. To talk things over. The day at work. The day at home. The children. How best to provide spiritual food for thriving young converts.

But the subject that was uppermost in both of their minds soon came up. Brought to the surface by Liz this time.

"I must tell you about a story I read the other day, George," she began. "I think it might help us in this problem. It said something to me."

"Let's hear it. Quick." was George's eager reply. He was certainly keen to hear anything that could shed any light up the dark tunnel of the future.

"It was about a ship. A sailing ship," Liz went on. Encouraged by the reality of her husband's interest.

"A Christian missionary was travelling on this sailing ship. Heading for America or somewhere like that.

He had to attend a very important meeting on a certain date but he was sure that he would never make it because they were very much behind schedule. There had been hardly any wind for a couple of days and the ship had almost stopped. It was becalmed.

During the voyage the captain of the vessel had often

chatted to the missionary. Had come to respect him. And his belief in the power of prayer.

The captain himself was becoming concerned about time being lost. He had an approximate timetable, which he was expected to keep to. Besides, some of the passengers were growing restless.

He asked the missionary to pray that God would send the wind. To speed them on their journey.

The devout Christian, a man of prayer, agreed. He instructed the captain, "You go up on the deck and order the crew to put up the sails. And I'll pray right now."

"Oh no!" retorted the astonished captain. "I'll not put up the sails until the wind comes. My crew would laugh me to scorn if I asked them to hoist the sails in a flat calm. They would think I was bonkers. When God sends the wind then I will put up the sails."

"I'm afraid I can't go along with that," said the servant of God, quietly confident. "That isn't the way God works. Faith must be involved here. I won't pray for the wind until you put up the sails."

"Well that's the end of that!" concluded the ship's captain, "I'm not going to make a fool of myself in front of my crew."

With that he left. Hurriedly.

Still the ship remained motionless. Not a ripple on the sea. Not a breath of wind. Nothing stirred.

There was stalemate between them.

Suddenly, unexpectedly, about five hours later, a less arrogant captain knocked the missionary's cabin door. Again.

On being invited to enter, he merely poked his head around the door and said softly, "The sails are raised sir."

"Good," replied the missionary. "Now I can begin to pray for the wind."

He started to pray there and then.
Soon the sails began to fill. With a gentle breeze at first. Then a stiff steady wind.

And they both fulfilled their appointments.
On time."
Liz paused to give George some time to reflect on the story.
He had enjoyed it. But he knew that there must be a moral in it somewhere.
Liz was too busy to tell long stories like that just to pass-the-while-of-an-evening.
She wasn't going to leave him in any doubt. As to what she thought it meant.
For them. In their predicament.
"Do you know what I think God wants us to do, George?" she enquired at length.
Having decided that the time was ripe for the manifestation of her intuition. "I think God wants us to take the first step. Make the first move. Having faith in Him. I think He wants us to put the "FOR SALE" notice up on this house and then He will send us on our way. In His will."
George saw it! Instantly! That was the answer to their problem. They were to put the house up for sale! And leave the rest to God.
It wasn't long until George set the wheels in motion. Got things moving. He knew it was the right thing to do. The proper course of action.
Hadn't God taught him months ago, under an old-fashioned lamp on the King's Road, "Just trust Me. That's all?"
Up went the "FOR SALE" sign on their house. On a pole in the front garden. And they had no idea whatsoever where they were going to move to. With their two young children.
But God had told them to do it.
They both believed it.
That was enough.
Before the "neat modem end-of terrace house" was advertised in the "Belfast Telegraph" the next evening, it was sold!
George and Liz's next-door neighbours were Christians. And friends.
Pat Kitchen, their neighbour, had a brother called Eddie

who had mentioned to him a time or two, "If you ever see a house like your own for sale up in that area where you live, let me know. I would be keen to buy one."

Eddie was planning to marry his girlfriend Eileen shortly, and was on the lookout for a house. "Somewhere decent, but not too dear," was how he had described his requirements.

When Patrick looked out of his bedroom window that morning he could hardly believe his eyes! There was a "FOR SALE" notice on a pole in the garden of the house next door. George and Liz's!

He didn't even take the time to get dressed! Pulling a dressing gown on over his pyjamas he ran out of the door, jumped the fence, and "bagged it!"

For Eddie and Eileen.

When Eddie heard of it later on that day he was delighted. Signed for the house. Paid for it. And it was his!

This proved to be a satisfactory solution to everyone's situation. Eddie had a house for his bride after they were married. Which wouldn't be for a while yet. He was in a position to wait.

George and Liz had obeyed what they had been convinced was the guidance of God in their lives. And He had known all along that the buyer wouldn't be demanding immediate possession of the property!

That nagging worry had caused George some restless moments and sleepless hours! Had held him back for months!

He was learning to take one step at a time.

Trusting God.

His neighbours couldn't really understand it. Selling out with nowhere to go.

Trusting God.

He was launching out into another phase of his life. And he wasn't even aware of it!

But he was trusting God.

Could there be any more stepping-stones to be crossed?

Over the swirling torrent of life?

Were there any more rungs on the ladder?
Up to the dizzy heights of the will of God?
He didn't know what was going to come next.
Hadn't a notion.
But he was trusting God.
He had to.

CHAPTER 22
Burning Rubber

Now they were in a real fix.

Had sold their house. Signed, sealed and settled. But still they had nowhere to live.

And it wasn't for the want of trying.

The days and weeks and months ahead were to take George and Liz up far more dead-end-avenues than it would be possible to recount.

They searched the "Property for Sale" ads. in local newspapers.

They followed up leads, which were messages and recommendations from the friends-of-friends.

They all proved fruitless. Pointless.

Straws in the wind. Wells without water. Dreams without substance.

One of the seemingly potential pathways took them as far as Dublin. But nothing came of it. As usual.

On another occasion they had actually reached the stage of having placed the deposit on a house. Only to be disappointed to learn that it had been sold to another customer a day or two later, for a higher sum.

When George's dad heard of that transaction he was enraged. Furious. "Listen son," he said to George, "I haven't much money, but what happened there was totally wrong, and I'll stand by you in this. Help you out the best I can. We'll fight them for it in court. All the way."

He really meant it. Mr. Bates, senior, was an upright man. Honest to the core. And he expected everybody else to be the same. If they weren't you challenged them. That was his code of conduct.

George understood his sentiments, but declined his offer "No, Da." he said, "Thanks all the same. But I'm not touching it."

"Why not?" was the amazed response.

"Because God has shut this door and no man can open it. We would only be wasting time. And money. If it's not God's will, I wouldn't want to live there anyway. If it had been God's will nothing could have stopped it. Do you know what I mean?"

His father nodded. "Yes, I know what you mean, George," he agreed. Time and experience had taught him something about George and Liz. They were different.

Things didn't just happen in their lives.

God made them happen.

And if they didn't believe,

God wanted them to do it,

There was no way in the world

You could drive them to it.

So he dropped the issue. Retired to the sidelines. But maintained his interest.

And let them get on with it.

So intent were they in procuring a house that they read every ad. in every local paper. And if it seemed reasonable at all, they followed it up. Or rather Liz did.

After George had left for work in the morning Liz set about her day's activity. Which consisted of clearing up the housework, and then setting out. She was off on her walking tour of Belfast. Viewing houses. Any houses that caught their attention. And they knew they could afford.

She walked for miles. Many, many miles. Pushing baby Daniel around in the tansad.

There came a time, after a few months of pushing, that Liz had to change the wheels on the tansad. She had walked so far, in viewing so many houses, that she had burned the hard rubber tyres right down to the rim! The metal was sparking off the pavements!

With it all, they still hadn't a house!

And the house they were living in wasn't their own. It was Eddie's. And Eddie was longsuffering. He had said that he wasn't in any great hurry. Eddie could wait.

But not forever!

Meanwhile, as Liz was engaged in all this walking, out at different times of the day, in all kinds of weather, George was very aware at the back of his mind that what she was doing was just a waste of time. And energy. He knew within himself, through his experience of God, that it wasn't going to happen that way. She could wear another set of rubber wheels to the rim and it wouldn't make a button of difference. She still wouldn't find the house that God had for them.

He didn't discourage her though. In fact he encouraged her in her buggy-pushing marathons. After all, it was good therapy. It was keeping her mind occupied. Her thoughts engrossed. Come to think of it, what could be better than a mile or two in the fresh air for herself and the children?

She was being spared the vexation of spirit that he was experiencing.

For him there had been many periods of prayer and fasting. Much calling upon God for guidance.

Still nothing seemed to be happening.

He had sold his house. He had trusted God. But now he was right at the end of a cul-de-sac. Where he couldn't even get turned round to go back.

He was stuck.

At last, one evening, George threw himself down before God in total anguish of heart. Sprawled flat out on the floor of the Lord's room.

He was frustrated. Disappointed. Confused. Recently he was beginning to feel just the tiniest little bit sore.

"Lord, what is happening here?" he cried out in his misery. "You definitely told us to sell the house. I just thought that you were going to lead us to a bigger one, at a rock-bottom price. Maybe needing a bit of work done to it. Lord, but we were ready for that.

You know all the red herrings that we have been chasing for months. As we have waited for You, Lord.

And You know, Lord, for You know everything, that Eddie and Eileen can't wait forever. They have been very patient. This just can't go on much longer.

I've done all that You've asked me to do. But You are not producing the goods.

Do You think this is righteous, Lord?

Please do something. Quickly, Lord. Quickly!

I ask it all in Jesus' Name. Amen."

When he had finished his agonised petition, he hesitated only briefly before drawing himself up.

Sitting down on one of the chairs, he dusted his knees. Straightened his clothes. Felt more satisfied. Less burdened.

He reckoned that God was in the corner again. He had put Him there he believed. There is no way out for God now, George thought. HE must do something for us. And soon.

In all these calculations, George had made one fundamental mistake. One basic error. And he should have known better. From experience.

He had grossly underestimated the speed of the Divine footwork. The heavenly capacity for a comeback.

Next morning, early, George was kneeling in the Lord's room. Yet again. Before an open Bible. He hadn't slept very well. so he got up to contact God. Through Scripture-reading and prayer.

As he read in the prophecy of Micah, his thoughts were arrested by the words, "the righteousness of the Lord." Wasn't that what he had been saying to God last night?

"Surely this couldn't be righteous, Lord."

To know "the righteousness of the Lord," the readers and hearers were exhorted to study Balaam's answer to Balak. (Mich 6 v. 5)

His curiosity was aroused. A desire to investigate further, spurred him on.

What was Balaam's answer to Balak? Where would he find it?

After some diligent searching he soon found the answer to his query. It was in Numbers. Chapter twenty-two.

"If Balak would give me his house full of silver and gold, I cannot go beyond the word of the Lord my God to do less, or more."

"What is this all about?" George thought. "Is this some kind of message about some kind of a house?"

Then he thought he saw the point of it. Something else he could say to God. Was God not soon going to take notice of him?

It was the second prayer of the verse that prompted George to voice his sentiments. To God. In prayer. Once more.'

"Isn't that what I have been trying to tell You, Lord?" he began. "I've done absolutely everything that You have asked me to do. So it's all up to You.

I can't go beyond the word of the Lord my God to do less or more.

I just can't do any more...."

There he stopped. In mid-prayer. The flow of words and thoughts dried up.

God was about to challenge him. Sort him out. Bring him down a peg or two.

It isn't possible to do any more, he had argued.

But was it possible, could it ever be possible...? God hit him with a thunderbolt. Could it be possible to do any LESS?

Was he attempting to short-change God?

"Are you trying to give God less than He is asking?

Do less than He is expecting?" The thoughts came probing.

George was indignant at this.

Hadn't he done as God had instructed? Hadn't he sold his house?

"Sell all that you have, and come follow Me"?

"I'll go back to the original verse," he decided. "Read it again. Just to satisfy myself. Set my mind at ease."

He knew the story well. Turned it up easily. Luke chapter eighteen.

What does the verse say? Running his finger down the page of his Bible he soon found it.

And read, aloud.

"Sell all that you have and give to the poor, and you will have treasure in heaven. Then come and follow Me."

To make doubly sure that he wasn't seeing things he read the verse again..."Sell all that you have and GIVE TO THE POOR..."

The colour drained from his face. A peculiar cramping sensation gripped his stomach. His knees began to shake, and the rest of his legs might as well not have been there.

He had been dealt a staggering blow. A knockout punch.

George collapsed on the sofa. In deep shock.

He was the one in the corner now. Slumped over the ropes. There was no fight left in him. He was on the verge of being counted out.

"and GIVE TO THE POOR......"

"How come I have never noticed those words before?" he pondered. Self-interrogation time again.

"I must have read that verse dozens of times."

On contemplating this latest self-directed question he came to understand the reason.

It was simple.

If he had realised what the whole verse said in the first instance, he wouldn't have set out on this road. Set sail from his own secure little harbour. Never.

God was levering him gently along.

Now that He had persuaded George to embark on this course of action, He was showing him the next stage of the process. The next phase in his development. The next command for him to obey.

Was this another step towards ultimate surrender or a final step to abject poverty?

It was definitely out of the question.

What does the verse say again? There must be some other meaning. Some face-saving interpretation.

Slowly and thoughtfully he read it. Yet another time.

Hanging on every word.

"Sell all that you have, and give-to-the-poor-and-you-will-have-treasure-in-heaven..."

Oh yes! That's what it says all right.

"Sell all that you have, AND GIVE TO THE POOR."

Was he going to have to give away all the money that had come in from the sale of his house"

......"and give to the poor."

Then the active mind raced on. Careering ahead. In defiant defence. He couldn't think of any reason in the world to give to the poor, whoever they were, except that this verse had said that he should. It would be simpler to come up with any number of practical reasons as to why he thought that he shouldn't.

His immediate reaction was, "What's to happen to us? Liz and the wee boys and me? Are we to give away everything that we've got and become gypsies? Wandering about begging for money and clothes. Making paper flowers and collecting scrap metal."

He visualised his first interview with his father. After he had given away all that they had, to the poor.

"Daddy, I wonder if you could put Liz and the children and me up for a night or two?"

"Certainly son. I would do anything to help you. You know that. But what's wrong with your own house? Have you not been able to buy another place yet?"

"No. We haven't bought anywhere yet. Daddy. And we won't be buying anywhere else either. You see we have donated all the money that we got for our house. To the poor."

George knew his father. Well. But he wasn't exactly sure what would happen next. His father would either faint on the spot or run away or run out or run off as hard as he could! The very least he would do would be to call his benevolent son either an idiot or a fool or a moron or all three combined and lots more beside!

No. He couldn't give to the poor.

The picture of Liz and he tramping the streets of Belfast with their few remaining possessions stacked onto a handcart, flashed graphically across his mind. One of the boys perched on top of the load. The other one helping to push. In his bare feet. It wasn't on.

Then he addressed God. For as he had been wrestling with this whole ridiculous demand, another question kept gnawing at his mind. Like a rat at an old rope. Eating into it. Fraying its edges.

It was this thing about "the poor." Who were these "poor" anyway? This was his escape hatch! It must have been only for Bible times this!

He said, "Lord, I would give to the poor if I could find them. But who are they?

Sure there's nobody poor now. What with the dole and the National Health. Help with your coal or your rent or your rates. There's nobody really poor now. Lord.

The only people who I could think of that I could ever describe as poor are the people who have drunk their money. They had plenty and now they have drunk it all. That's neither your fault nor mine. Lord. It's their own.

There's nothing much that we can do about it. Lord.

There is nobody poor nowadays..."

As George's mind continued in this vein, making excuses to God, there came an irrefutable answer. Like a stealthy whisper in a silent room. Like a stirring breeze on a sultry summer day. It came gently. But definitely. Into the mind, so determined to find an emergency exit, came the words of Jesus, spoken so long ago, but relevant forever because of their content - "The poor you have with you, ALWAYS."

Bang went another half-baked argument! Knocked on the head! There must be somebody poor! Somewhere. Jesus had said that they would be with us. Always. He could find them. If he would only bother himself to look!

In a further attempt to evade the issue, George made one

final last-ditch-effort. It was a practical question of logistics. Of distribution.

"Even I did want to give liberally to the poor. Lord, and even I did know who and where they were, how could I get the money to them? Wouldn't it only be money they would need?

I couldn't take time off my work. Lord, to go and dole it out, and there's no way that I would give it through some of these organisations. They would probably use half of it for administration. And if I was giving it I would want it to go straight to the poor. Not to them."

This was his last shot. His ultimate feeble excuse. He knew it wasn't enough. It would never satisfy God.

He ended up in a confused condition. Totally perplexed.

It was like being in a canoe. On a fast-flowing river. Without a paddle. Heading over a waterfall.

He wished he had never launched himself on this voyage of faith.

"Sell all that you have..."

He had done that. The first big push-off from the shore of security. He had sold his house.

..."and give to the poor......"

That made him want to give up. Renege.

Jump out. Abandon ship.

But he couldn't!

His mind, his intellect, the whole common sense of his existence kept repeating. Sometimes in a shout, sometimes in a whisper, but always in earnest

"I can't! I can't! I can't..."

Yet every time he restated his intransigent position-every time he said "I can't!" an echo came back in exactly the same tone as he had used...

It travelled all the way out into the timelessness of eternity, and returned deep and booming with the vastness that surrounds an Almighty God...

When he shouted, the echo shouted back.

When he had whispered, the echo whispered back.

There was only one difference. The wording was changed.

When he called out, "I can't! I can't!"

The echo called back, "I know. But I can. If you will trust Me!"

Whatever was he going to do?

CHAPTER 23
A Special Dispatch

There was a mental block involved here now.

An impasse.

Of course their bountiful Lord could have everything and anything that His grateful followers possessed. Even to the extent of the proceeds from the sale of their house, apart from the small sum that they owed to a Building Society to make it entirely their own.

Hadn't He given them everything that they had ever had in the first place?

But they were scared.

Afraid of over-zealousness. Afraid that through misinterpreting some fluky series of events coupled with the reading of coincidental Bible verses, they would make a big mistake. Run on ahead of God and mess up the machinery of His will. Find out, when it was too late, that God hadn't been leading them that way at all.

"It would be completely different," George mused one evening, during the course of one of his frequent reveries on the subject, "If the Lord Jesus was actually standing physically beside me in the living-room telling me from His own lips what to do.

I definitely wouldn't hesitate then.

Or if I could lay the whole thing at an apostle's feet. But then they are all in heaven.

There is the chance of an element of human error. With so much at stake.

What if I'm wrong and I make a total fool of myself? And my wife and family. And worse than all that, bring the Lord's

Name into ridicule. Make an absolute laughingstock of all those I love, and everything I believe in."

Having concluded that it would be unwise to do anything rashly, or take any leaps in the dark, he decided to put the entire matter on hold.

Kneeling in the Lord's room once more - in a quandary again - George poured out his heart to God.

"Lord, I pray the half-way prayer," he commenced.

"If this is pure unbelief and fear and disobedience, then I can't change my attitudes and emotions at will.

But I want to be willing to do Your will.

And I'm willing to be made willing.

Lord, please make me willing to be willing.

For Your Own Name's sake.

Amen."

Having finished his prayer, he left it there.

With God.

If God could make him willing, then he would be willing. Fair enough.

Meanwhile he had to go to work. Every day. In Spar. And on some occasions, at peak periods, he was asked to stay on after normal closing time. To work late into the evening. To cope with the rush. Or clear a backlog. The wee bit of extra cash in his pay packet was always welcome. He had a wife and two growing sons to feed. And clothe.

It was during one of these overtime stints that he had his first real conversation with Mr. Henry Holmes.

This Mr. Holmes had a part-time job in Spar. It was a trusted position. He managed the place when the daytime managers had gone home.

Since the overtime shift was worked with a skeleton staff Mr. Holmes turned his hand to everything. And enjoyed it. He checked over stock and checked out loads. His final duty of his evening shift was to make sure that the warehouse was prepared for the next working day.

On this particular evening he called George across to him.

He had just finished checking out a load that George had been working on. Driving a forklift.

When he had switched off the truck, George hopped down and walked over to where he was standing. Dwarfed by a massive-mini-mountain of bulky cases of cereals.

While he was still approaching, but Mr. Holmes reckoned that he must be within normal-tone-earshot, for he opened the conversation. Without any preamble. Straight to the point.

"A remarkable thing happened to me last night, George. I think you would probably be interested to hear about it..."

His surprised-and-somewhat-at-sea listener was right beside him now. Mr. Holmes was continuing.

"For no apparent reason whatsoever, I awoke in the middle of the night last night. One second I was lying fast asleep. And the next I was wide-awake. This was peculiar. There had been no bumps or bangs to waken me. As I lay there wondering why I suddenly felt so alert, a thought clearly impressed itself on my mind. It was about you George..."

By now George was beginning to feel slightly uneasy, wondering what was coming next. He hadn't long to wait.

"It said, 'Tell George Bates about David Ravey.' I immediately fell into a deep sleep again. And slept like a log until the morning."

Sensing George's mild embarrassment, Mr. Holmes gave him a moment or two before enquiring, "Have you ever heard of Mr. Ravey, George?"

To this question the answer was straightforward. George just replied quite simply, and honestly, "No, sir."

With a sort of a chuckle to himself, Mr. Holmes looked down at the floor. He had a pure white moustache, which caught the light. A fashionable little hat with a feather in it was doing its best to cover his thatch of pure white curls. A few had escaped and were peeping out. Sneaking out to the light.

"I suppose that's a silly question anyway." He laughed as he spoke. "For if you had already heard about him, what would be the point in me telling you."

George had always thought that there was something imposing, almost awesome, about this ageing gentleman. He knew that he had travelled extensively and had at one time been a Member of Parliament.

Up until this moment, however, his only communication with Mr. Holmes had been to do with their work. About loads and lorries. About cases and cartons. It was just a trifle unnerving for him now to find himself suddenly sharing in the thoughts and experiences of someone whom he had respected so much. From a distance. For so long.

"Well," continued Mr. Henry Holmes, "as a member of such a large Christian meeting as the Victoria Memorial Hall, it has been my privilege very often to entertain speakers from all over the world. But if you were to ask me for the name of the man who lived closest to the Biblical description of a Christian, out of all the men that I have ever met, then without hesitation I would have to say David Ravey."

"He must be some man, sir," George replied. Not quite sure what to say.

"He is indeed," went on Mr. Holmes, his sincere expression adding weight to his words. "A man who lives by faith in God. David left a thriving business behind to work among disabled people. Helping them in countless ways. Even to the extent of bringing them into his own home. Looking after them. Without charge. It never costs them a penny. Yet David makes no appeals for money. And he refuses to go into debt. He just simply looks to God to provide for all the needs of the work. And for the needs of his wife and family. And his own personal needs as well."

There was a pause. Both of them looked around and then

back to each other again. "Well what do you think, George?" Mr. Holmes prodded. "Are you going to do anything about this?"

George was taken aback by the directness of his approach.

"No sir, I don't think I can," he responded cannily. Thinking carefully. He had other problems on his mind. But yet he didn't want to appear offensive. Or even ungrateful.

"Just for the moment anyway. I would prefer to leave it with God. Pray about it in the meantime," he continued. "You will understand what I mean when I tell you that I am already praying for direction about another matter. I would be afraid of making a wrong move. Taking a wrong turn. Acting without definite guidance. It would be so easy to make a mistake. And I can't go in two directions at once."

Mr. Holmes understood. He was a kindly Christian gentleman. He nodded his head, smiled, nervously readjusted his little hat, and resumed his work. Back to the check board with the pen.

A day or two later, George, Liz and family had been invited to dinner at the home of their friends Jim and Greta Moore. At Ainsworth Pass on the Shankill Road.

After the meal, while the ladies were clearing up and talking about curtains and children, home and heartaches, Jim suggested to George that they should go for a walk. A dander round the streets. Clear their heads and give them the chance to have a chat.

George was delighted at the prospect. Not that he was particularly fond of walking at that time but he would be glad of the chance for a chat. He relished the opportunity to share with Jim something of the Henry Holmes experience. He wondered if Jim would know anything about this David Ravey. Would he ever have heard of him?

They walked around the streets off the Shankill Road. Up one street and down the next. Past rows of neat little houses with shiny letterboxes and painted window-sills. Past children swinging around lampposts, playing hopscotch or kicking half-flat balls to each other in the street.

George and Jim were too engrossed to notice much about their surroundings. As they were walking they were talking. Or rather, more correctly, George was talking. Recounting the whole story to Jim, the man who for so long had been his spiritual mentor. Whose advice and opinions he had always respected.

Jim wasn't getting much of a chance to talk or advise now, however. Just to prove that he was still listening he would pop in with a grunted "Uh-huh" now and again.

Otherwise George did the talking. Told him everything about his conversation with Mr. Holmes. He thought Jim would understand. And he was right.

Jim understood. He was fascinated by it all. And he was pleased to learn of the depth of commitment to God's work and His will that there appeared to be in the younger man's life.

"What are you going to do about it George?" he asked, when the story seemed to be finished.

"I can't touch it Jim, until God shows me His will. I don't want to take any chances. Make any mistakes," George replied, wondering to himself why both men he had been talking to were both so convinced that he should be "doing something about it."

"Yes, I see what you mean," said Jim, directing George across towards a telephone kiosk on the opposite side of the street.

Entering the kiosk he half-turned to George and went on, "Step inside with me here a minute, George. I have a call to make but I'm not sure of the number off-hand. I'll have to look it up in the book." With that he took the dog-eared, cigarette-butt-scarred, drink-tin-ringed telephone directory down from its precarious position on the little ledge where it stayed. "Just you keep talking there."

In a very short space of time Jim found the number that he had been looking for. And dialled it. George had been doing as he had been instructed - he was continuing to chat away.

The line was clear and after the ringing tone a cultured voice said, "Randalstown 421. Can I help you?"

Jim responded with, "My name is Jim Moore, sir. Is that Mr. David Ravey?"

George's mouth fell open in astonishment. Total surprise. He had no idea that Jim was going to do this.

"It is indeed. David Ravey here," came the reply from the other end of the line. The startled George whispered into Jim's only available ear, "What are you doing Jim?"

The whispered question was completely ignored. Jim was concentrating on the task-in-hand. He felt it was important.

"Mr. Ravey, I would like to introduce you to a friend of mine called George Bates," he said, and with that he removed the receiver from his ear and thrust it into George's hand.

To say that George was flustered would be to grossly understate the situation. He was utterly thrown off balance. Flummoxed. His mind went blank. Words wouldn't come. He felt that he had never even learnt to talk. Yet he had to say something. The last thing in the world that he wanted to do was offend this gentleman about whom he had heard so much.

"Mr. Ravey," he stammered, not knowing just quite what was going to come next himself. His mouth was opening and closing like a clockwork frog's. "I live up in the Castlereagh Hills and there are a number of us meet in a room in our house to read the Bible and pray. We call the room the Lord's room."

"Yes?" The voice-from-Randalstown seemed intrigued. Inviting him to continue.

"Many of these Christians that come up to our house were once drug-addicts and drop-outs. I have been hearing recently a little about the kind of life that you live. And the work that you do. I was thinking at first that perhaps you could come and speak to us sometime."

George held back again. He became conscious of the fact that possibly he was asking this busy man to do something that he would consider unimportant. Trivial.

"On second thoughts," he continued, "I'm sure a man like yourself would be more interested in addressing big meetings. It would hardly be fair to ask you to come from

Randalstown to Belfast to speak to our small group. Don't worry about us."

Gracious man that he was, David Ravey set him at ease straightaway, in his deep strong voice. The warmth of the tone of a man whom he had never met encouraged George greatly. And his response encouraged him even more.

"Oh no, George, no!" he responded. "Please don't think of me like that. That's just the sort of meeting that I love to be involved in. Talking the Gospel. Right amongst the heart of the people. Just exactly where they are at. I would be absolutely delighted to come."

A date and time were set.

The receiver was replaced.

David Ravey was on his way!

CHAPTER 24
Enter Elijah

The intervening days, between the telephone call and the prearranged date, were days of speculation for George.

What would this person, about whom he had heard so much recently, be like? Would he fit in with the people who met in the Lord's room? Would they get on well together? He had certainly been reassured by the man's voice on the telephone, but would he be so encouraged when they met?

When this unique servant of the Lord, David Ravey, did come as planned, he brought a good friend of his with him. John Laughlin was his name. The evening thus turned out to be a double treat. Two for the price of one! A really special event. A realisation above all expectation.

George and Liz were entranced, as were all who were present that evening, by the stories that David Ravey had to tell. Every eye was fastened on this tall, well-dressed gentleman as he recounted something of his experiences with God. He often interspersed his sentences and phrases with a winsome smile, and his eyes twinkled with reality and delight as he warmed to the purpose for which he had been invited -relating how God was at work in his life. He told of the ministry among the disabled folk and some of the wonderful evidences of God's guiding through difficult situations.

This man fascinated George. Held him spell-bound.

The younger man began to realise, as the minutes and hours of the evening rushed unnoticed past, that here also was a man who had known the mighty hand of God operating purposefully in his life. In a supernatural way. The only difference was that David had been having these deep and definite dealings with God over a longer period of time.

There was some extraordinary similarities between the practices of the tiny group meeting in Randalstown, and themselves. George was fascinated to take special notice of them one by one as they became apparent.

On Wednesday nights they listened to the ministry of Willie Mullan on tape. And on Friday nights they met to pray.

On Sunday mornings in Randalstown they met to remember the Lord. Using grape juice and unleavened bread.

Their group did not see themselves as having any denominational tag. They just wanted to live as close as they could to the Bible pattern. As they understood it to be revealed in the New Testament.

As David continued to narrate the way in which God had led him step by step throughout his life, and the beliefs of his close group of Christian friends, he wasn't aware in any way of what had been happening in the Lord's Room, Glenview Park. But George was.

He was amazed. Stunned almost. He didn't think that there was another group in Northern Ireland quite the same as theirs. Yet here was a man, in his pleasant deep voice telling them of one. Almost exactly the same!

Later on that evening, over a cup of tea and sandwiches they all came to know each other a little better. A friendship was ignited that was to kindle into a flame of comradeship and respect, and a common desire to see Jesus Christ, their Lord and Saviour, glorified in their lives and land.

As David and George shared with each other their uncanny encounters with God in their past years, this man from Randalstown, a total stranger up until that night, impressed George by his personality and prayers. He must be something like Elijah was, he thought. Continually in touch with God. About anything. Everything. He lived in contact. The lines were always open.

While others were exchanging views on the episodes that had been recounted, John Laughlin would occasionally interject with a, "Yes, that's right" or, "It sounds incredible, but it's true." This quantity surveyor from Stormont was sincere and genuine in his faith. His life also had been touched by the testimony of David Ravey.

George couldn't help thinking that John was a remarkable Christian in his own right. Like Barnabas in the Bible. "A good man, and full of the Holy Ghost." In his unspoiled humility he seemed to be totally unaware of the positive influence that his open and upright living was having on others.

All involved that evening, the Lord's Room regulars, the Randalstown visitors, and George and Liz, the well-satisfied conveners, revelled in the congenial atmosphere of the occasion. It was approaching midnight when the rejoicing group reluctantly decided to disperse.

It became clear before he left, however, that David Ravey had been as deeply affected by George's life and testimony as George had been with his.

Although their character, their life-styles and their backgrounds had been poles apart, they were to discover that they had vitally important common ground. In-depth encounters with Omnipotence. The tentative thread that was thrown out in an impromptu telephone call, was to develop through the cords of Christian mutual respect, into a mighty mooring rope that was to anchor them together in their work and witness for God.

George and Liz stood waving "Goodbye" as John and David set off to drive back to Randalstown. As they turned to walk down the path back into the house after the car had disappeared, George remarked to Liz, with complete conviction, "I'll tell you this Liz. Mr. Holmes was definitely not exaggerating. Everything he said about that man was absolutely true. Dead right. Spot on."

A man of God had entered their lives.

CHAPTER 25
The Sticky Sixpence

An evidence of the bond that had been forged between them was the fact that David and George were drawn into meeting again.

This next social contact was one evening a few weeks after that enjoyable initial encounter. There was no audience this time. No formality. It was a-getting-to-know-you-and-yours kind of an evening.

David and John travelled from Randalstown to visit George and Liz, bringing Claire, David's daughter with them. David was keen that they should meet her, and so she was introduced.

Claire was a qualified nurse, and a dedicated Christian. It soon became evident to George and Liz, as the evening progressed, that she was possessed with her father's non-stop capacity for work and his in-depth compassion for the disabled.

They chatted amicably around the fireside in the living room, over the inevitable cup of tea. As they talked they were dwelling on the theme that was often to characterise their conversations in later days. A dream of revival in Ireland. Of people experiencing God in a real, deep and tangible sense.

When they recalled God's dealings in their own lives George voiced the sentiments of them all as he said, "If only we could let Ireland see what our eyes have seen. God is alive and moving on planet Earth. He can change hearts and lives Even countries if we would let Him."

David set his tea-cup down on the saucer. As he looked across at George the firelight was reflected in his glasses.

He spoke as a man with a mission. He had a burden on his mind. This was the time to share it, he reckoned.

"George, do you believe that it is God's will for Christians to have a holiday?" he asked.

This was a surprising question. It seemed to be breaking across every train of thought that they had been enjoying. They had been talking seriously about seeing Ireland won for Christ. Not going on their holidays!

It was a simple, straightforward question, however. And George had a simple and straightforward answer. It was obvious to him.

"Oh yes, I do," he replied at once, "After all didn't the Lord Himself say to His disciples one time, 'Come ye yourselves apart and rest awhile.'

Was that not a kind of a holiday? A break anyway?"

That was exactly the answer that David had been anticipating. It had been a leading question. And George afforded him the perfect opportunity to unveil his vision.

"That's true, George" he responded. He looked solemn yet serene sitting there. It seemed as though he was drawing the thoughts and words from some secret inner recess of his person as he continued, "But what about the physically afflicted people? Poor people who aren't able to go on holiday. Probably couldn't afford it anyway. Many of them are Christians. What about them?

And what about their families who are committed to caring for them. Day in, day out, week in, week out, for years on end. They never get a holiday either. Never a break.

What about people with multiple sclerosis for example? Or blind people? Any kind of physical handicap you would like to mention. What about them?

Is it not God's will for them to have a holiday?"

David sat right back in his chair. This action seemed to indicate that he had finished. For the meantime, at least.

The hushed silence was broken only by gurgling water in the pipes somewhere.

Slowly George was coming to realise that something big

and heavy was pressing down upon the mind of this man of God. He knew that David was opening his soul to them.

"Of course, far more so," was his considered reply. "I believe that God would definitely want them to have a holiday too."

"Well now," David began again. He was a very sincere and deliberate man. Time and talent were too precious to be wasted with him. He even used words to their best advantage.

"I agree with you George. And I am praying that what God is doing in my life in a small way, with the disabled folk in Randalstown, He will do in a much bigger, greater and more marvellous way. And if I don't make appeals for money, but look to God alone to meet all the needs, then Ireland -and the world -will see what our eyes have seen. Realise what we all know from practical experience. That God alone can meet every need. That He can work powerfully and wonderfully in lives. Changing and controlling, guiding and directing, providing and protecting. That He indeed is great."

Their conversation continued late into the evening. Sharing dreams. Comparing visions.

The three from Randalstown were loath to go home. But it had to be done, so they went.

After they had left, George and Liz sat down by the fireside again. It was time for reflection. That sort of pleasant end-of-the-day, too-much-on-your-mind-to-sleep kind of feeling.

George poked and raked at the dying embers to stir up a last glimmer of heat.

They both realised that they had seen "the writing on the wall."

God had wakened a man up in the middle of the night. To move him to tell them about David Ravey. Then David Ravey had come and told them of the burning desire of his heart. To expand the work of the Lord amongst the afflicted. So that God would be glorified and the poor would be blessed. So that those who couldn't afford a holiday could have one. So that those who perhaps had never ever had a holiday because of physical incapacity could enjoy one. And all in Christian surroundings.

They sat there quietly. Enjoying each other's company. Savouring all that had been discussed. And there was much to contemplate.

George could sense that Liz was tiring. She began to show signs of ready-for-bedness. He felt compelled to express what they both felt.

"I believe that this is God letting us know who the poor are. And where we can find them," he said.

"He wants us to give the money to this work that David is planning. Whatever it turns out to be."

"You're right, George," Liz agreed. She too had been convinced during the course of the evening that they had found the poor about whom they had been seeking guidance from God.

And He had revealed it to them. In His own mighty and marvellous manner.

But the realisation of the truth brought its attendant problems. As it so often does in life.

Between the recognition of the truth and taking action upon it.

There falls the shadow.

Between knowing what you should do, and actually doing it – there lies the dilemma.

Oh yes, George and Liz were fully persuaded that they ought to offer the money to help in this particular and specific vision of a provision. For the poor and the physically handicapped.

As the days passed by and they boiled it all down to pounds and pence they knew that it could be tough. It was going to be hard to let go of the natural. To trust the supernatural. That money represented all that they had. And to give it away, to provide for the poor, however deserving their need, with no obvious replacement, was going to require one tremendous step of faith. It would be like Peter. Stepping over the edge of the boat. To have a go at walking on water.

In his hesitation to take the necessary action, George compared himself to a wee blind boy. Standing holding his sixpence pocket money tightly. In a firmly clenched fist. Beside him a generous gentleman was whispering, "Open your hand, son." He wanted to put a ten-pound note in it. The child gripped his sticky, sweaty sixpence all the tighter. Determined not to let it go.

Here was God wanting to bless George and Liz. Abundantly. And they were blocking Him out. Unintentionally.

Late one evening George was lying on the sofa in front of the fire. Liz had gone early to bed and the children were asleep. The house was quiet.

He was pondering his problem.

As he gazed fixedly on the hearthrug, his eye caught the length of its edge.

"That's the span of your life," his thoughts seem to tell him. "But you don't know exactly where you are positioned on it. You might be only halfway through or you could be almost at the end. You could live until you are a hundred and fifty or you could die tomorrow. You don't know. But in whatever length of time there is left, you will never realise the full potential of God's plan for your life, unless you choose to obey Him.

With all your heart.

And with all you have.

And now."

The message was clear. The hand must be opened.

The "sticky sixpence" would have to go.

CHAPTER 26

The Wonderful Wednesday

Since George and Liz had been convinced of the will of God for their lives, but hadn't acted upon it, they began to notice something. They became aware that they didn't have the power in their Christian lives that they used to have. They had lost their sparkle. The gloss had gone. The lustre was lacking.

God was as faithful as always and George was fully aware that service was a voluntary thing. Nevertheless, he was keen to know God in his life. To the full extent of Almighty Power. Second best, half-way-measure, would be no use whatsoever.

As he arose one morning he was so burdened about this that he felt his heart would break. He was weighed down with worry, because God didn't have absolute sway in every nook and cranny of his life. He must bring this spiral to a climax. One way or the other. It was Wednesday, 24th February, 1971.

Over breakfast he poured out his heart to Liz. Only to find that she was of the same mind. They had to do something about it. Together.

Although he was already late for work, every other consideration seemed to pale into insignificance as they entered their own personal sanctuary. George and Liz bowed down on their knees, side by side, in the Lord's room.

A Divine stillness pervaded the place. Liz took one of the white scarves that were neatly folded and left available for the convenience of visitors, from a chair beside her. She covered her head.

It was a sacred moment. They were on holy ground.

"Lord forgive us for holding back," George began, praying earnestly on behalf of them both.

"But You know how serious and far-reaching the consequences of this decision could be. But Lord, we would rather have Jesus than silver or gold. Although we don' t know what way Your hand is leading us, we offer it all to You. The money is Yours to do with as You will. From now on, Lord. Not only in theory, but in fact.

It may not be much in other people's eyes. But as far as we are concerned Lord, it is all that we have. We are scared in case we should make a wrong move.

We believe that You have shown us clearly that it is to be given to David Ravey for his ministry among the afflicted.

Bear with us. Lord, and grant us a token, if it be Your will. We are not tempting you. But please make our paths cross in some way. Would You somehow bring him to us.

Please show us Lord. Where - and how - and when - we should give him this money.

We ask it all in Jesus Name. Amen."

As George finished praying, he trembled. That prayer represented a total resignation to the will of God. By both of them. They were confident that God had heard their prayer. And would answer it.

An impediment was removed. An avalanche of peace flooded their souls.

They were prepared to go all the way with God.

Rushing out to work, George was euphoric. And as the day wore on he was conscious of a special sense of the presence of God. He felt that God was so close that he would only have to stretch out his arm in any direction and he would touch Him.

It was George's custom to get away on his own for fifteen minutes each day during the lunch break. To commune with God. Sitting in some obscure corner of a warehouse. Behind a stack of cartons of soap-powders. Or up the stairs in the little printing room, which was always vacant at lunchtime.

On this particular day he was reading from Isaiah Chapter 7. He was arrested by the words in verse fourteen.

"The Lord Himself shall give you a sign."

He took that as being a direct answer to their prayers. At eight o'clock that morning, Liz and he had asked God for a token. Now he was assured that it was on the way.

God was at work. Things were moving quickly. All at once, it seemed. At last. They would just have to wait.

After tea that evening, George was standing at their large living room window. Hands clasped behind his back. Peering idly through the Venetian blinds out onto the front garden.

Pat Kitchen was passing on his way home. George gave him a friendly wave. As he always did when he saw his neighbour.

With a returned wave of the hand. Pat beckoned on George to come out. It appeared that he had something to say to him. Some message to pass on.

When he went out to the door George greeted him with a genial, "How are you Pat?"

It was clear that Pat had something on his mind. He wasn't his usual, happy-go-lucky, "how's-about-ye-George?" kind of self.

"My brother Eddie told me to ask you if it would be possible for him to have possession of the house by the end of March. That is, only if that would be O.K. with you and Liz," he said.

It was obvious that he was glad to have that bit over.

"No problem at all. Pat. That's fantastic! And tell Eddie that we deeply appreciate all that he has done for us. Letting us stay in the house for so long," George replied.

He was enthusiastic outwardly. Blown to bits inwardly.

He had been waiting for a sign from God. But he had expected it to be good news! Now here he was, telling Pat that it would be "no problem at all" for them to be out of their house in five weeks time. With nowhere to go! Were they going to be out on the street? Without a roof over their heads?

Pat held on to one of the cement posts and threw his leg over the wire fence, into his own garden next door.

George closed the door and went up the hall. When he entered the living room he found Liz in a state of shock. She had heard the conversation at the front door. Her face was pale.

With a tremor in her voice she inquired anxiously, "What are we going to do? Now we have no money OR no house. Where are we going to go?"

Although his own knees were knocking and his stomach was churning, George knew that he must reassure her. As best he could. Kneeling down on the floor beside the chair where she was sitting he held her firmly by the shoulders. He looked into her eyes. Apprehension and care were written in there. He could read it easily.

It was a tense moment for both of them.

"Liz, love, I know exactly how you feel," he said, comfortingly. "I am shaking too. But we mustn't give in to that kind of thinking. We are leaving God out of the picture when we think like that. We must believe that He is going to meet our need within the next five weeks. Eddie wanting into the house has put a date on it. The end of the line is in view. At last."

Brave words. Consoling words. The right words. But did he believe them himself? Away deep down, in that hidden part of him, that only God could touch?

Rising from his position on the floor he reached for his Bible. Which he always kept close at hand. He felt unarmed without his "Sword", as he called it.

In need of something to stabilise him, to restore his own confidence, he opened the well-worn pages. His eyes fell upon the command,

"Cast thy bread upon the waters." Ecclesiastes 11, verse 1.

George's faith revived when he read that verse. Everything that he had read that day was relevant to the immediate present. Not five weeks away. And his bread was his money. He and Liz had consciously, deliberately and unitedly cast it upon the waters. That very morning.

"That's it, Liz," he decided. "God is going to do something tonight. I'm away to get changed."

He was still in his working clothes. But if something was going to happen he would need to be prepared for it. Dressed up in his one-and-only suit.

Liz was still so weak that she couldn't get up. She was powerless. Speechless. Numb.

What is he talking about now? She wondered.

"Get changed?" she repeated. Puzzled. "For what? Are you going out somewhere?"

Disregarding her questioning, George went upstairs and washed and changed. Groomed himself up as he said he would.

Waiting for something to happen.

About nine-thirty Liz said to him, jokingly, "Would you look at him! Sitting there all dickied up to the nineties. With nowhere to go."

"Just you wait," George smiled at her as he spoke. "The night's not over yet."

At ten o'clock there was a knock at the front door. Liz looked up from her knitting, surprised.

"What did I tell you?" was her husband's simple response to the look of bafflement that crossed her face.

As he walked down the hall to open the door he felt like a child at Christmas. Excitedly opening a gaily-wrapped mystery present to see what he had got.

What had God sent him? Or who?

He opened the door in one sweeping movement.

There stood David Ravey. Holding a briefcase.

"Excuse me calling so late, George," he began. Then he stopped. He was hesitating. When he noticed the style of George, he was sure that he must be interrupting something very important.

"I don't want to interrupt you," he continued. "Are you going out somewhere?"

"No, I'm not David, but we have been expecting you. We have been waiting for you all evening. The Lord told us that something was going to happen."

George's face, and his heart, were aglow.

David looked mystified. Nobody knew his whereabouts. How could they have been expecting....

"What?" he stammered.

"I said we have been waiting for you all evening," repeated George, grabbing him by both arms to pull him into the hall. "Come on in. You are very welcome."

David came into the living room. And greeted Liz. Who was just as bamboozled as he was, but she tried not to show it. Hadn't she poked fun at George for getting all dressed up? Now this - David on the doorstep.

After general introduction time, "give-me-your-coat-till-I-hang-it-up" time, David sat down in the armchair below the window. Liz was sitting on the sofa at his right-hand-side.

George didn't sit at all. He stood. Opposite David. With his hands clasped behind his back, again. Not gazing dreamily out the window this time though. He was agitated. Uneasy. Restless.

"I thought I would just call and see you when I was passing this way...." David was explaining. Liz appeared to be interested in what he had to say. At least she was smiling pleasantly, and nodding her head.

George didn't hear a thing. Not a word of it. His heart was thumping loudly in his chest. There was a roaring in his ears. Like a train thundering through his head.

A powerful conviction from God was troubling him. "You said this morning that you would give David Ravey the money you got for the sale of this house. For his work among the afflicted," it reminded him.

"You asked God to make your paths cross. And to show you where. And when.

Well here he is. Sitting in front of you.

And it's here.

And it's now.

Or you are going back on what you said this morning."

Suddenly the soliloquy was shattered. He was jolted back

from far-away self-harassment, into the reality of the here-and-now.

David was addressing him. Asking him some question or other. And he hadn't even the foggiest notion what it was about.

"I'm very sorry David," he confessed, "but I haven't heard a word of what you have been saying."

"Oh that's all right George," the gentleman replied, "Don't worry about it. I'll start again...."

"No don't. Please don't," George stopped him. "There is something that I know I have to say to you."

It was David's turn to put the brakes on.

"Hold it George," he interrupted. "You're not going to tell me anything until we have prayed, brother."

David stood up. Closed his eyes. Bowed his head. Raised his hands to heaven.

"Lord, close George's mouth if what he has to say is not from You," he prayed. It was dialled direct. Straight to the Throne.

When he had pronounced a quiet "Amen," he looked quizzically across at where George was still standing. Transfixed. Rooted to the spot.

"Now do you still want to tell me that thing? Whatever it was, George?" he probed, gently.

He had resumed his seat. But he was sitting on the edge of it. Expecting George to make the next move. And he did.

His action was prompted by Liz, who had produced a little Building Society book from her handbag. She knew too, what George was going to do. What they both had to do.

He took the book from Liz as she held it up to him. Then taking a couple of steps across to stand in front of David, he said, "David, we have sold our house. And this is the money that we got for it.

The Lord has told us that we are to give it to you for your work among the disabled people. To do with as the Lord leads you."

David was silently shocked. Dazed but delighted, all at

one go. He sat quietly for a moment or two, then he spoke to Liz. He was anxious to make sure that they were both equally committed to this unique step of faith.

"You have obviously talked this over at some length," he remarked.

"Oh yes, we have indeed. We are both in it," Liz assured him.

Holding the Building Society book almost reverently in his hands, as though he had just received it, recorded delivery, from a member of the heavenly host, he asked, "Where are you planning to move to then?"

He looked from one to the other, through narrowed eyes, as he spoke.

"We haven't a clue David. It's all in God's hands now. We are simply trusting Him to guide us," George replied calmly.

That deep inner peace, that closeness to God, had returned. Liz and he had shot the rapids, and were now adrift on the placid waters of a tranquil lake.

"Well," said David. "There is something important that I must tell you now. Nobody is allowed to read my diaries, George. But I want you to take my diary out of my brief-case over there...." He nodded across to where it rested. Propped against a corner of the sofa. "And read the entry for the seventh of January please."

George opened the briefcase. Rather hesitantly and somewhat clumsily. He was so agog with nervous excitement that all his fingers felt like big toes.

He had expected to find a small personal diary, of the slip-it-into-your-inside-pocket variety.

"That's it there," David indicated, pointing to what looked like a logbook.

George turned to the appropriate date and read aloud as instructed. So that Liz could hear..."January the seventh.

Lord, if George Bates is the man you want to live in our home in Randalstown, please show us clearly. Cause a gift of one thousand pounds for our work amongst the disabled to come through him, as an indication that we should give him our house."

After the reading was finished, David explained to the by-now-mesmerised couple that he believed that God was presently taking possession of a home for the afflicted. A place where that greater, mightier work for Him that they had talked about many months ago, could commence. And develop.

And the Lord had already told him, very definitely, that he wasn't to sell the property in Randalstown.

He had therefore sought the Lord's guidance as to who should occupy the house in Randalstown after he would move. And God had indicated to him very clearly that it was to be them. George and Liz.

David had passed on thousands of pounds to the needs of others in his lifetime. He knew from experience the reality of God's promise that if you give it shall be given unto you.

So he put out a seemingly impossible fleece. This was to be the sign. God would cause a gift of one thousand pounds for his work amongst the disabled to come through George.

This was going to take some kind of miracle, he had reasoned. David was convinced that George wouldn't have a thousand pence to his name. Not to mention one thousand pounds!

Imagine his absolute astonishment when he realised the amount of money that he had just been given!

God had gone beyond what he has asked. Far and away beyond anything that he would ever have dreamt of asking.

He had been given back -through George and Liz -through the Building Society book, which he was passing lightly from one hand to the other - the equivalent of all the money he had ever given away! To God and His work.

Staring blankly at David, totally dumbfounded, George asked, "David, what exactly does all this mean?"

His mind was whirling. He must be careful. Cautious even. It would be foolish to read too much into the entry in his friend's diary.

"What I believe it means is that we will be on the move before long. To a bigger property. To expand and develop the work that God has led us into," David replied enthusiastically.

"So the house in Randalstown is yours, George," he went on. "Carpets. Curtain. Fittings. The lot. It's all yours. The pair of you."

Liz's eyes and her husband's met. Waves of emotion flooded their hearts. They were overwhelmed by love for Christ who had Masterminded this miracle.

They began to wonder. Is this all a dream?

Is this for real?

George couldn't restrain himself. He shouted, "Praise the Lord!"

Tears ran down Liz's cheeks. George hugged her warmly. They had been close together as they ploughed through the storms of trepidation. Now they were equally close together as they floated on clouds of rapture.

A sense of gratitude. Of thankfulness. Of relief. Had taken over in their once turbulent minds.

After their elation had reached its highest elevation and they began to sink gently back towards earth again, George regained his composure.

Turning to David, who had been momentarily forgotten, he enquired, "By the way David, where is this big holiday home for the afflicted that you have bought?"

"Oh, George, I haven't bought any place yet," David informed him coolly.

"You've just got the money but you haven't decided on which property to buy. Is that the way of it?" George was eager to hear more.

He was playing for time. Trying to get this whole situation figured out in his head.

"No," said David. Never ruffled. Ever polite. "I'm afraid that I haven't got the money to go and buy a holiday home. I wish it were true."

At that moment George came out of orbit. His gradual

earthward descent ceased. He plummeted down and hit the ground with a sickening crash.

"David, do you not think that was cruel?" he asked quietly.

"What do you mean George, - cruel?" David was startled. "I don't understand."

"Well David, put yourself in our position for a moment" George began to explain, in a low voice.

His deep disappointment was hard to disguise.

"We have just been informed tonight that we have to be out of this house by the end of March. We have kept our promise to the Lord and given you the money. But we were secretly wondering what was going to happen to our family. Where were we going to go?

Then you clear it all up for us. You tell us that God has told you to give us your house in Randalstown.

We were caught up in the excited belief that our need had been met. Only to find out now that it hasn't.

Our hopes are dashed again. We were flying high. Now we are smashed to pieces!"

"I'm confused, George," he said. "What do you mean? What is your problem? Your need has been met, brother."

"But we can't take your house if you have nowhere to go!" George protested vehemently. "That's what I mean!"

"Oh I see now!" David replied with a chuckle. "Is that all that's worrying you? I assure you, brother, that I have something better than property or money. I have God's word for it. That He is going to meet our need.

Don't you realise yet, George, why you had to give away all that you had before God met your need? You were exercising faith, brother. Faith in God.

Now if you had to give away all that you had before God met your need, why shouldn't I have to give away all that I have before He meets mine?

You understand what I mean, brother? I must exercise that same faith in the same God. For without faith it is impossible to please Him...."

George stopped him again. He felt he could soften the blow. Blunt the cutting edge of the "Everything Must Go" commitment.

"It may be God's will for us to have your house, David," he said. "But we certainly don't need your furniture and fittings. We still have our own bits and pieces."

Liz and George were almost speechless with joy. They had been encouraged by David's strenuously held belief that God was working His purposes out, in all of their lives.

Spontaneous gratitude led them to thank God, and His servant David, time-and-time again, for the well-nigh-impossible events of that day.

As he rose to go, David lifted his briefcase and fastened the catch.

Then he spoke the final words of that wonderful Wednesday.

"Look, I'll arrange for the pair of you to come to Randalstown some day next week," he said.

"To see your new home."

CHAPTER 27
Storm Brewing

True to his word, David did arrange for George and Liz to go to Randalstown to see their new home. On the Saturday of the following week. Sixth of March.

They didn't have a car yet. So David came up and collected the excited couple. They were all dressed up and ready to go when he arrived. A dream was coming true for them!

As they journeyed they talked of many things, including a seven day fast in which the two men were involved at that time. They discussed the simple praise service that they had held the previous week in the Lord's Room. To mark the great deliverance that God had worked in the lives of George and Liz.

The conversation had been light-hearted. Friendly. Refreshing. It was great to be together again. They had always so much to talk about whenever they met. Wherever they met.

Suddenly David's tone seemed to change to a more sober note. It was so quick. Inexplicable, almost.

"There's something I feel that I must tell you, brother," he began in that characteristic way, to which George had by now become accustomed.

Without giving the young pair any time to adjust to the change of mood, he continued, "I can see a parallel between the children of Israel and ourselves. It has impressed itself deeply on me recently. Especially even this morning before I came to collect you."

David was driving along steadily and unloading his burden gradually.

"Do you remember the story in Exodus chapter fourteen? How that the children of Israel had come out of Egypt. Only to find themselves in a no-go situation. They were in wit's-end-corner. Hemmed in by mountains, pursued by enemies and halted by the Red Sea."

George was nodding and smiling. He knew the story well enough.

"Can you remember, as terror filled their breasts, what happened next?" David asked.

He paused for a moment.

"Yes," said George. "Moses was commanded to stretch out his rod. And the Red Sea opened. To let them through."

"Ah," David gave a quiet, knowing laugh. "That's just what I thought you would say. But there was something before that, George. Something that it's possible to miss. You see, the Lord caused the sea to go back. By a strong east wind all that night. A storm, George. God sent a storm. I'm sure the children of Israel wondered if God was for them or against them at that point. As they huddled together, listening to the wind howling round them.

But God used that storm to open up the sea. And the way ahead for His people."

George and Liz listened to David's thoughts on the children of Israel. And their predicament. The Red Sea. And a storm. But only with half-an-ear and fifty percent concentration. Strong winds in the Middle East thousands of years ago didn't worry them too much. They were on their way to see their new home. And they were thrilled about that. It was uppermost in their minds at that moment.

David went on patiently, with his gentle word of warning. "I believe, George, that we are heading into a storm, as we wait for God to work for us. I don't know what that means in practical terms, but whatever it is, the storm will open up a way. For us to go forward. I'm telling you this now so that you won't panic when it happens."

Becoming aware that a subdued hush had fallen on the car, David rounded off the explanation of his premonition with a final, "Just remember, George. It will be through a storm that we will go forward."

The tone changed back again. To a more relaxed, out-for-a-run-on-a-Saturday-afternoon style.

"Enough of that," said David. "This is a happy moment for you two. And here we are in Randalstown."

The car was just passing the gates to Shane's Castle.

Liz's eyes grew larger as she took in the size of their new house. It was built of solid stone. There was a garage at the bottom of the entrance lane. And beyond it a beautiful lawn and flower garden.

As the car drew to a halt on the concrete yard at the back of the house, the young couple saw for the first time, the little Meeting House in Randalstown.

A flush of expectancy filled them as they were ushered graciously inside that house. To be shown around. By David and Berta.

The evening was happy. Pleasant. Enjoyable. As they went from room to room, taking plenty of time about it, they were filled with emotion.

The months of waiting had been well worthwhile. The days and nights of anxiety had been unnecessary.

God is faithful.

As Liz measured up the windows in her eye for curtains, trying to work out what would fit where, George was trying to decide which would be the most suitable room to use for a study. But they were both experiencing a distant but definite doubt feeling in the depths of their minds. A feeling of this-can't-be-happening, it isn't-really-trueness. A feeling of being in a fantasy realm. A dream world.

But it was real. It was true. They hadn't just imagined it!

God is faithful.

After an appetising meal, and as they prepared to return home, George felt a very strong and definite constraint to tell Berta that she shouldn't come with them. The thought seemed so absurd that he was afraid to voice it. He didn't want his generous hosts to suspect that he considered himself to be super-spiritual.

So, with difficulty, he let it pass.

Away they went. All four of them. Back to Belfast.

David and Berta left later to travel back to Randalstown, and George and Liz went to bed. But not to sleep!

They had so much to think about. And talk about! And plan for! They were on a high.

Next morning they were delighted to tell their friends who had gathered to worship in the Lord's room, of the miracle that God had worked for them. Providing them with a new home, bigger than their present one, in Randalstown.

Needless to say, the families on both sides were relieved for George and Liz. That they, at last, had found somewhere else to live. They had considered the whole episode rather strange. Now they were beginning to wonder, "Is there something in this Christianity business after all?"

That Sunday night, George and Liz had just drifted off into a contented sleep, when there was a rattle at their bedroom window. Somebody was throwing little pebbles at it. Obviously trying to wake them up. Without disturbing the children.

Then the front door was knocked. Gently. Whoever it was had moved around there now.

"What time of the night is it anyway?" George wondered to himself as he stumbled out of his bedroom. Into the Lord's room, and across to a window.

He opened it. And peered out. To see who it was.

A man was standing at the bottom of the garden. Looking up.

It was Jim Moore. "Is that you, George?" he called. "I felt I ought to come round and tell you that there's been an accident, brother. David and Berta crashed on the way home last night. A car crossed the road and collided with them. A woman has been killed...."

George stopped him. He needed to hear more about this.

"Hold on there a minute, Jim," he interrupted. "I'll come down and let you in."

By now he was trembling with cold and shock.

After he had come in, and they had made themselves slightly more comfortable, Jim told George that David and Berta had both been seriously injured. And were in different hospitals.

The gravity of the situation began to register in his mind as Jim proceeded to describe the extent of their injuries.

"Berta's tongue has been slashed and her arm is broken. She is in a state of deep shock."

It was clear that he had been shocked as well, as he went on, "David is even worse. His leg is badly injured and his ribs are crushed. They don't know whether he's going to live or not, George." The storm had broken.

CHAPTER 28
Clouds Clearing

The news was devastating.

George just had to go and see his friends. Visit them personally. Help them, or comfort them, in whatever way he could.

He went into work on Monday morning and told the manager the whole story.

Although he was acutely understaffed that day - having six men out - he nevertheless agreed to let George off in the afternoon.

His mind was in turmoil as he travelled to Antrim. What was he going to find? Would they be as badly hurt as Jim had said? Or worse?

After asking for a few directions from the staff, he eventually found Berta. In the Masserene Hospital. Sitting up in bed.

She was badly bruised. Her broken arm was in plaster. And her tongue was cut. She had stitches under her chin.

And yet she smiled. And spoke.

She had lost none of her elegance.

Her serenity in the circumstances was a witness to all. She was totally at peace with the will of God for her life.

George was touched. As he looked at her, he wondered, "Does she know how badly hurt David is?"

He didn't know himself. But he was soon to find out.

Bidding Berta a tearful farewell, he left Antrim and went on to Ballymena. Where he found David. In the Waveney Hospital.

His prayer-partner was in a critical condition. He had a shattered pelvis. One of his knees and a foot had been crushed. An urgent operation was required, but the doctors were unable to proceed with it, because of his broken ribs. Causing respiratory problems.

As he gazed at his mangled frame George remembered his conversation with Jim Moore the night before, and asked himself over and over again, "Is he going to die?"

Nobody knew the answer to that question at that moment. Neither the doctors. Nor the family. Nor David himself. Nobody.

Only God. He knew. And His servant's life was in His hands.

Although he was in that terrible physical condition, David appeared eager to talk. His breath came in short painful gasps as he tried to reassure his friend.

"Don't-worry-George," he panted, with difficulty. "It's-only-the-storm-I-told-you-about...."

He closed his eyes to rest. George's eyes filled with tears. He was almost overcome with grief and emotion.

"Don't talk please, David," he said. "Don't try to talk, brother. Just rest. Take it easy there."

George paused to let David rest again. His thoughts and feelings were all churned up. Images of Saturday flashed across his mind. Thoughts from Saturday burned into his brain.

"A storm, George. God sent a storm...."

"I'm telling you this now, so that you won't panic when it happens...."

When David reopened his eyes, George spoke to him again. Softly.

"Is it O.K. if I pray for you, brother?" he asked.

David gave a small nod of assent. It was all his agony would allow. But he welcomed the prospect. His partner-in-prayer, in prayer for him.

Standing there at the end of the bed, George offered a simple child-like prayer of faith. Looking to God for the apparently impossible. Healing for David. This gentleman of God.

Being assured that he was resting wholly in the power and promises of God, George left. And returned to Belfast in the train.

David did eventually have a complete operation to reset his broken bones. On Friday, the nineteenth of March, in the City Hospital, Belfast.

Totally unaware that the crucial operation was in progress, the group in the Lord's room were engaged in fervent prayer. With one accord. The whole night through. For David. That very Friday night.

The atmosphere was charged with the presence of God.

They felt that instead of letting their friend down in a bed through the roof to the Lord, they were actually lifting him up in a bed through the roof.

Up to heaven. Up to the Lord.

It was only later that they learnt that the operation had been performed. And had been a total success.

David was going to be well again.

God had answered their prayers.

Coinciding with the heart rending, prayer inducing, events of those days, there was reactivated in George's mind a background turbulence. Like shingle rattling and shifting in a heavy tide.

From the moment that Jim had broken the news of the accident, there was this bewildering question. It kept rumbling away. Appearing. Diminishing, but never dying. Then reappearing. Grinding away at his spiritual confidence.

"What happens to you now? David and Berta are both all smashed up. They will probably be crippled for life. They're going to need their home in Randalstown. And one thing's for sure. They will never be able to take over any home for the disabled. Big or small. Anywhere.

You're back at square-one, George."

These fears were to be allayed by a telephone call. George phoned Berta one evening to enquire how she was. She had been discharged from hospital, and was at home in Randalstown. Convalescing. On the mend.

"George, I was wondering when you and Liz were planning to move?" she enquired. "For you are badly needed here now."

The house in Randalstown was really two houses. Joined together. So there was room for the Bates family in one half of it. And the Raveys in the other.

It was thus decided. They would move to Randalstown. Soon.

In early April they flitted. George, Liz and their two young sons. Lock, stock and barrel.

From Belfast, where they had lived all their lives.

To Randalstown, that they knew precious little about.

City slickers to a country-town!

As news spread throughout Northern Ireland, and beyond, of David Ravey's accident, many Christian hearts were stimulated to meet his need. Gifts were sent to him from concerned friends. From all over the world.

One Wednesday evening, George and Jim Moore were standing by his bedside. Although he was still in hospital, his condition had greatly improved. He was rejoicing in the goodness, kindness, and preserving care, of his bountiful God.

With heartfelt infectious enthusiasm he told them of a letter which he had received just that morning. Pledging to him sufficient funds to put a deposit on a large property in Donaghadee. "Wayside," it was called.

David was convinced that the Lord had indicated to him that this was to be the property, which he was to develop as a home for the afflicted.

It would be eminently suited to the purpose. It was spacious and well appointed. There were large function rooms in it. Many bedrooms. Ample bathrooms.

God had not only provided the necessities required for such a venture. But he had thrown in a few luxuries as well!

There was a beautiful chandelier, which when lit, could be seen by ships passing the Copeland Islands. And an outdoor heated swimming pool!

God's miraculous provision had gone far beyond their wildest expectation. Yet again.

The vision that he had cherished for so long, of a home for the disabled, was now becoming a reality.

The storm was abating. The Red Sea was opening. The mists were lifting, from the way ahead.

When David was well enough to leave hospital, George and he shared many happy times in prayer and fellowship together. In their two-houses-knocked-into-one in Randalstown.

There was just one dark cloud that gathered, and threatened to burst, dampening the closeness of that contact. It was caused when George discovered that the title of the bank account, used by the Christians from the Meeting House, implied a denominational name.

This completely cut across the deep spiritual convictions that had brought him thus far, concerning church unity based on truth.

It represented a crisis situation for George and Liz. Their principles meant a lot to them.

After much prayer, George approached David about it.

However, from the time he had come to know George, and his firmly held views on unity, David foresaw that this throwback from a previously failed attempt to form a fellowship would be a stumbling block to him. He had discussed it with a mature Christian who agreed that this title, which they had merely used as a convenience, should be dropped.

David, George and John Laughlin met and prayed together about the issue. And with much grace the problem was resolved.

The previous title was discarded.

The old was gone. And a new church had been established. Soon elders were recognised, and deacons appointed.

More settled weather returned. The menacing storm had blown past. Without dropping its deluge of rain, or causing any structural damage to that firm friendship.

On the eleventh of September, David and George sat chatting about the things of God. As they often did.

David shared with George an assurance that he had been given, as he had read the Bible that morning.

He had been reading in Jeremiah chapter forty-two, and verse seven. Where "the word of the Lord came to Jeremiah in ten days time."

"I believe, George," he stated, with calm confidence, "that this means that in ten days time I will be given the keys to Wayside, in Donaghadee. So that I can proceed with this holiday home for the disabled that we have been praying about."

George cringed at this. David was allowing himself room for disappointment. He had come out into the open with his positive affirmation. Had he let his left hand know what his right hand was doing?

This was unusual for David. A departure from his normal code of practice.

On former occasions he had prayed quietly and secretly. And God had rewarded him openly and publicly.

Now he had come out with it. God was going to give him possession of a beautifully appointed home in ten days time.

What if he was wrong?

The Devil would have a great laugh at him.

George was worried. He couldn't bear to see David hurt. Spiritually. His confidence shaken. Surely he had taken enough with the accident?

Voicing his misgivings only to Liz, George spent an anxious ten days.

When the twenty-first of September came, David appeared edgy. From early morning. He was unable to rest.

George winced inwardly as he watched him pace the floor with the aid of his stick. One leg was still stiff and he trailed it a little.

Up and down. Up and down.

With nervous excitement, he examined the post when it arrived. There was nothing of any significance there.

No deeds. No documents. No key.

Off he went again.

Up and down. Up and down.

The frustrating thing was that nothing happened.

The phone didn't ring. Nobody called.

As the morning wore on towards noon, George began to feel deeply sorry for him. He prayed silently that David hadn't overstepped it this time. Left himself a sitting-duck-for-Satan.

Just after lunchtime the phone rang. At last. Who would it be?

David rushed across to it. As quickly as he could. Picked up the receiver. George couldn't help hearing the conversation.

David's end of it. From his half-of-the-house. Both through-doors were ajar.

"Yes, Jim, and where are you?" David was asking in his polite-business-like manner.

"In London. And how are you going to get here?"

"You're flying over this afternoon...."

"Right then. I'll meet you at the solicitors...."

"Thank you, Jim. Goodbye for now."

When he heard the receiver being replaced, George went over to the door. As he opened it wider, David met him. His face aglow.

The edginess had gone.

The composure had returned.

"Well, that's it, brother," he began, trying to be as matter-of-fact as possible. But there was no disguising the suppressed elation in his voice.

"I have to meet Jim Allen, the present owner of the property, at the solicitors later on this afternoon.

To pay the deposit. And pick up the key.

To Wayside!"

The home that had previously belonged to Cyril Lord, carpet magnate, was now destined to be used in the work of The Lord of All.

The clouds had all cleared away.

The sky was azure blue.

But there had been a price to pay,

A storm which he had to pass through.

The strong east wind had blown all night.

For many, many nights.

But God had brought him safely through.

And out on the other side.

The winning side.

Wayside!

CHAPTER 29
Leaving The Nets

Three days later, on Friday 24th September, 1971, David, Berta and family moved out. Moved on. Moved up. Into the work that God had called them to do. The establishment of a home for the disabled. In Wayside, Donaghadee.

It seemed peculiar for them at first. The relocation was difficult. The change from a small compact house in Randalstown, to a large luxurious mansion in Donaghadee, took some getting used to.

There was an even heavier responsibility on David. Up until that move he had just his own family to look after. Now he had to provide for a flock! He intended to open this home as soon as possible. For the blessing of a continuous stream of needy people. And to the glory of God, whom he was confident would meet every need.

The family proved ideally suited to the work, and soon adapted. Both Berta and Claire were trained nurses, and another daughter, Dorothy, left her position as catering manageress in a Christian holiday complex, to come and help.

Meanwhile, back in Randalstown, life progressed as usual for the Bates family. They too had acclimatised easily to their new environment.

George travelled by bus every day to work in Spar (John Henderson Ltd.) As forklift driver. He welcomed that journey in the bus. It afforded him an hour each way to rest. And reflect. And commune with God.

As Christmas 1972 approached, George and Liz were to receive a most precious gift. Their third son, Nathan Robert was born. On 12th December.

Jim Moore and Jimmy Evans were now employed in the huge British Enkalon factory in Antrim. They thought that it would be great if George could get a job there too. Why should he pass it every day in the bus, to go to Belfast? When it was just down the road from where he lived?

They were so preoccupied about this proposition that they made it a matter for prayer. When they met each other briefly in the lunch-hour. To pray and study the Bible.

A third member of their prayer group, called Brian, had been given an extra application form, when requesting one for a friend.

They took this as an answer to their prayers.

And brought it to George. Who filled it in. And sent it in. George was duly called for interview, and was offered a job. Doing shift work. But he refused it. Because of the staggered pattern of working.

He was busily and happily engaged in caring for the little assembly of Christians in the Meeting House. And he wanted to be free in the evenings, and at the weekends, to further this involvement.

When he had declined the offer of a job doing shift-work, he was offered a day job. Eight o'clock until five o'clock. Five days a week.

"Mind you," the Personnel Manager warned him, "The pay's not nearly as good."

Although the pay was only about half of what he had been getting in Spar, he took the daytime job.

He knew that if it was in God's will he would lack nothing. And he didn't.

After he had taken up his position in that factory, George realised that God had been leading him there. He saw it as a mission field in itself. An island inhabited by three thousand people. Many of whom were in need of salvation.

During the years that he worked there, he had the privilege of leading at least eighteen people to faith in Christ. In the back of container-lorries. On locker-room floors. Or wherever they could pray in private.

Away from the hustle and bustle of work. And into the presence of God.

One summer evening, when George, Liz and family were on holiday in a caravan at Sandycove, near Millisle, Co. Down, David Ravey called round for George. To take him to a meeting.

A friend of David's, called Tom Hamblin, from the Sands Soldiers Mission in Singapore, was to be the speaker at a meeting of the Worldwide Missionary Convention. In Rosemary Park Baptist Church, Bangor. David was very anxious that George should hear him.

Tom Hamblin spoke of the need "to go in and possess the land." For the life of faith demands it.

He graphically portrayed a Christian life that just goes round in circles.

Ever moving. Going nowhere.

When all the time there is so much fertile land. Just waiting to be possessed.

George was enthralled. The message captivated him.

Tom leaned over the pulpit. Pointing into the packed congregation he said, "If you are willing to go in and possess the land of God's will for your life. No matter what it is. Then stand up right now! Just where you are!"

George jumped to his feet. Stood to attention. Like a soldier on a parade ground.

Although he was no exhibitionist, and had no desire to make a fool of himself in public, he had been spontaneously catapulted into a standing position.

The speaker's fiery eyes immediately intercepted him.

"You have no doubt what you want, sir! That's for sure!" he said. Speaking directly to the still-stiff-standing George.

There was a rustling all around the building.

Others were beginning to rise.

On returning to the caravan later, George found Liz still up. Waiting for him. He knew that God had done something more in his life. Was demanding more from him "A possession of the land." Whatever that meant.

And it had all been so unexpected.

"Liz," he began, as they settled down for a chat. "How much have you in your purse, love?"

"I don't know George," she replied. "But I'll go and look if you like. I haven't very much. But what do you want it for? Why do you ask?"

"It's just like this, Liz," he went on to explain. "God challenged me in that meeting tonight. And all I know is that something has happened to me. But I don't know what's coming next. I could be called out of my work to serve God, or anything."

He lowered his voice.

"And I don't mind telling you. I'm frightened!"

Liz knew to look at him that he wasn't exaggerating. God was moving in his life once more. She had been through these experiences with him before. And knew the telltale signs.

So she left it there.

For three days after that, George sensed the presence of God enveloping him. His mind was alive with expectancy.

But it faded. Died away. Choked by legitimate cares. A home. A family. And a thriving church.

For months there was no move forward. Except for one occasion when the voice of God clearly spoke to George. Challenging him afresh.

It was through a message that his fellow-elder, Jim Pedlow, preached one Sunday in the Meeting House. About Abram neglecting to obey the call that God had given. Those thoughts loomed and thundered through his soul. Causing him to weep uncontrollably for an entire day.

But that was all. A mere fleeting blip on his spiritual radar as he continued his voyage. Diligently and conscientiously. Round in circles.

It was Liz who was to speed things up. Bring him back to the borders of the land.

Arriving home from work one evening, when "possessing the land" was far from his mind, George noticed that she was obviously more prepared than usual for his arrival.

She was uneasy. It was clear that there was something she wanted to tell him.

As they were sitting round the table having their meal, Liz said, "George I want to warn you about something. I'm not trying to be cheeky, but I feel I have to warn you..."

George wondered what he had done. What was coming next?

"I was before the Lord this morning. Having my quiet time. And for some reason I cried and was broken before the Lord," she continued. "I dedicated my life to Him anew. And told Him that if He wants us to live for Him in full-time service, then I'm ready, with the three children. To go out now."

There was little that George could do. Or say. Just listen. This was God. Another time.

Liz had almost finished. "I prayed that God would speak to you and bring you out. And I believe that I have to warn you."

This sudden insight into the depth of his wife's commitment to God, and to him, came as a shock to George. And it never left him.

From that moment the Spirit of the Lord didn't let up in his life.

You must go out. Possess the land. Labour for the Lord. Step out in faith. Now.

Wave upon wave of messages from the Lord bombarded him. With increasing rapidity. But still he was uncertain and afraid. The old story all over again.

"What if I make a wrong move here? If I get it wrong this time it's not just for a week or two. It's for the rest of my life!"

Listening to a tape one Wednesday evening with a group in the Meeting House, God confronted him once more.

Willie Mullan was the speaker. As always.

Sitting there with the others, pondering this question of serving the Lord in a full-time capacity, Reason took over in the mind of God's would-be-servant.

"Lord, there's a single man over there," his reason argued. "Able to preach and teach. And if You would only call him out to your work he would just be one mouth to feed. But if You call me out You will have five. You'll have to provide for Liz and the three boys as well."

Sounded logical enough. Good economic common sense.

As his mind turned in again to the voice-from-the-tape, he was startled to hear a verse that penetrated, and then shattered, all his feeble arguments.

It was from Genesis chapter fifty.

The speaker said, "Now therefore, fear ye not. I will nourish you. And your little ones."

You. AND your little ones.

That was it.

The voice of Christ was saying "Follow Me."

George would have to leave the nets. And go. And follow Him.

God would provide.

Thus it was that on Monday 21st April, 1975, at exactly 8.00am. George walked up to the charge-hand's desk in British Enkalon, Antrim.

"Victor, I would like to give in my notice," he said. Calmly and resolutely.

Victor was taken aback.

"What do you mean, George? You must be joking. You're one of our best workers. Have you got another job somewhere?"

"No, Victor. I haven't got any other job anywhere. I'm going to serve the Lord full-time."

He knew it would be difficult to explain his heartfelt, God-given conviction to a non-Christian foreman.

"Do you realise that if you give in your notice now then you'll have to leave on Thursday night. Think it over. Until after lunchtime, at least. If you don't give in your notice until this afternoon then you will have to work two week's notice. That will give you time to make sure that you're doing the right thing."

Victor felt obliged to explain a few things to this respected, but rash, employee.

"No, Victor." George's response was immediate. "I believe that God wants me to give in my notice here and now. I want to obey Him. And as soon as possible."

Pat Kitchen had preached in the Meeting House on the previous morning about Abraham. Rising early in the morning, to obey God.

"God requires instant obedience," he had said.

George had decided that his God would have it.

When the news spread, as it did, like wildfire, around the factory floor, his workmates thronged over to him.

"Is it true that you believe that God has called you to do this?" they enquired.

"What's this we hear about you giving in your notice, George?" they asked.

"What about your wife and family. Who's going to look after them?"

The questions, and comments, showered in thick and fast.

"Your head must be cut!" somebody growled. Half-jeering, half-sympathetic.

"What will you do when you have no money? Will you go on the dole?" was one of the more common jibes.

"You'll have to go and beg for help if you don't!" they continued.

George held up both hands. Trying to silence the torrent of taunts. Craving permission to speak.

"I can assure you all that I'll do neither. Go on the dole, or beg. For if I didn't believe already that God could keep me off the dole, I wouldn't be leaving my job in the first place..."

Having been given this chance to clear up a few points, George was making the most of it.

"And I'm not going to make any of my needs known to anybody, so I won't be begging. Even if we are all starving...."

One big fellow stepped forward from the crowd that had gathered around. Interrupted George.

"Then we will be burying you within a month!" he forecast. "And your wife and family with you!"

Many heads nodded in agreement. "That's true," they were all thinking..."Bates is crazy."

George turned and looked big Jim in the eye. "Be reasonable now Jim," he said in an even tone. "You know as well as I do that I'll have a lying week. And my holiday pay. We could all survive for more than a month on that..."

The crowd had gathered a crowd. More had joined on at the fringe. To hear what the commotion was about.

By now he was entirely surrounded. Shifting his attention from Jim alone, George addressed all the men. Fearlessly.

"But I'll tell you all, this. If any of you see me. Or my wife. Or my children. Within three months from now...

Then you will know that there is a God who lives.

And who is able to provide for his people!

And you need to get right with Him!"

CHAPTER 30
My God Shall Provide

The year of 1976 had its heartbreaking moments. It was in that year that George lost his mother. A mother, whom he had loved and respected, passed away. To be with Christ, who had graciously saved her soul, twelve weeks before she died.

In addition to George's grief at parting with his mother, Liz had her share of heartache. She lost her father. John Miskelly. The man who had carried "the bullets" down to the shipyard.

He had been impressed by the remarkable change in the life-style of George and Liz. So much so, that as a result of their witness and testimony, he too came to know their Saviour. Shortly before he died.

Their best friend was also to be called home to his reward in 1976. David Ravey died early in the year. The work that God had led him into, in Wayside, Donaghadee, still continues. Capably managed by Andrew Erwin and Claire, who became his wife.

God had an Elisha. To replace his Elijah. And He still provides for His servants.

These were times of proving God's ability to comfort in sorrow. And supply every material need. For George and Liz. Aaron, Daniel and Nathan.

Since George had left his employment, over a year ago, they had been amazed at the variety of methods that God had used to provide for them.

They had learnt to live in a hand-to-mouth situation. For they had been delighted to discover something wonderful.

It was God's hand. And their mouths.

In the summer of that year they decided to go on holiday. Get away from it all. They had been pressed to the limit in the

My God Shall Provide

rapidly developing work in Randalstown. A change and a rest would be most welcome. And the children deserved a holiday.

When the day came to set out on their long-awaited holiday, they crammed as-much-as-it-could-hold, into their second-hand, white-where-it-wasn't-rusty Renault 5. George's parents had bought that first car for them. And the whole family loved it!

So when they had packed their belongings into it, they packed themselves into it! And off they went! All five of them.

Driving through Newtownards, George remarked, "This is great, love. Nobody will know we are on this wee holiday. We will get peace for a couple of weeks. To enjoy the children. And one another's company!"

"Yes, George, it's great," his wife replied. She too was looking forward to their holiday. Perhaps even more so than he was, since she had put in a lot of planning and effort to get them to that moment.

But she felt that she ought to make him aware of something. That only she knew. She worried in case he would get too "carried away."

"Do you know, George, we haven't a lot of money at the minute," Liz began. Breaking the news gently.

"We will just have enough to buy potatoes every day. There will be no trimmings. Meat or vegetables, or anything like that. Just potatoes," she went on. Spelling it out in terms of food-on-the-plate-for-five.

George was unmoved. Undisturbed.

"Don't let that worry you, love," he replied. "Won't we have each other? And the boys. It will be like angel's food. Those potatoes will taste like manna from heaven. You'll see!"

Liz smiled. As long as he was happy, she could be happy.

The tumbledown house near Donaghadee, in which they had booked to stay, was a hide-away. Not a holiday chalet.

It had one room up. One down. No flush toilet. No running water. It was beside a busy main road, but was barely visible to the passing motorist because of an overgrown and under-cared-for hedge.

The rent was to be 50p per week. A snip, even then.

As they were unpacking the car, and the children were running around excitedly, exploring every nook-and-cranny of the house and garden, a knock came to the door.

George left a box down on the nearest available uncluttered spot. And went to answer it.

A young boy stood there. About five years of age. He was holding a plastic shopping bag in his hand. Nearly as big as himself.

The face was familiar. It was Victor's son. From Newtownards.

"My mammy was passing in the car," he said. His bright eyes were alight. "And when she saw your car in here, she asked me to run in. And give you this."

It took both hands to reach the bag up towards George. Who didn't take it immediately. There was something mysterious about this.

"But how did she know we were here?" he thought aloud.

"We purposely haven't told anybody where we were going!"

He turned his attention to the child, who was still holding up the bag. Patiently. But the arms were beginning to shake.

"Tell your mammy. Thanks very much! She is extremely kind," he replied, at length. With that he took the preferred bag, and the child disappeared through the hole in the hedge, whence he had come.

As he walked back into the house, George held up the bag. Opened it. Peeped in. He was so grateful to God when he found that it contained meat and garden peas.

To go with their potatoes!

And that was just the start.

The two weeks of their hideaway-holiday were filled with similar miracles. They hadn't told anybody where they had planned to go, and yet they never lacked anything.

Bacon and eggs. Tea and coffee. Fresh fruit and vegetables. Ice cream and jelly. All arrived on their doorstep. Courtesy of their Heavenly Father, who had undertaken to provide. And didn't seem to need a forwarding address!

On the journey home, George could hardly contain his joy.

"Liz," he said. "If someone had give us five hundred pounds before we came on that holiday, we would have missed out so much. That was a holiday with God."

He noticed that Liz was quiet. The boys chattered away in the back seat. But there was an uncanny silence in the front. Did his wife not share his exuberance for the holiday which they had just enjoyed? He could have been sure that she had loved every minute of it.

"Are you not feeling well, love? Is there anything wrong?"

George was concerned. He knew that there was something amiss.

"No. No," Liz replied, assuringly. "I'm every bit as grateful as you are, George. I couldn't agree more. But to be honest, I have been praying secretly to the Lord about a wee thing. And I thought He would have done it for me."

She sounded mildly vexed.

"What was it?" George enquired pointedly. A bit taken aback that Liz had a secret.

When all was revealed, it turned out to be a very simple problem. But the sort that a mother would worry about.

"Well, it's just this," she began. "The school is going away to camp tomorrow. And I will have to pack for Aaron soon after we get home…"

Her voice dropped to almost a whisper. "And there's a big hole in the sole of one of his training-shoes. The rest of the kids will all have nice new ones. I was just asking the Lord if He would give us a little bit extra. To get him a pair."

George was struck dumb. And his heart was filled with a sense of shame. He had failed as a father. A son of his was through to the sock!

This was a challenge. How was he going to provide this basic requirement for his son?

Hadn't God promised to provide for him and his little ones? Did that promise extend to training-shoes? he wondered.

Deciding that there would never be a better time than the present to find out, he swung the car into a shopping centre.

At Clandeboye. On the Bangor ring road.

"Where are you going, George?" It was Liz's turn to be pointed now. "Have you got money that I don't know about?"

"No, I haven't Liz," her resolute husband replied. "But we are going in here for training-shoes."

Ignoring the weird looks that she was giving him, George went on to explain his reasoning. "I'm not tempting God. But He has already given me His promise. To provide for my little ones. The promise of God is better to me than the signature of the President of the Bank of England on a twenty pound note."

As he stopped the car, Liz decided to make her position clear.

"There is no way that I'm going in there with you. You are going to make an absolute fool of yourself. And you can if you like. But I will not be with you."

She said it. And she meant it.

"But Liz, I need you with me...." George's powers of persuasion were about to be tested.

"To tell me Aaron's size, and the colour you would like. You will have to come with me!"

So it was that George coaxed and half dragged his extremely reluctant wife into the shopping centre. And over to the racks of training-shoes. Though he didn't have enough money to buy a pair. And neither did she.

"Look," Liz half-whispered to George. "That girl's not serving anybody. And if I go over there and lift a pair of training-shoes she will probably think that I want them. And expect me to pay for them."

"Liz, just do it!" George insisted. "Or I will never know what to do in this position, if it ever occurs again."

"Right!" she said, provoked. She took a few determined steps forward. To her this wasn't living by faith. It was just sheer stupidity.

It only took her a matter of seconds to find Aaron's size. And choose a suitable colour.

Lifting a pair from the shelf she rammed them into George's stomach.

"There!" she announced. "That's Aaron's size! And here comes the woman!"

At that precise moment a voice said, "Brother George, and what are you doing down here?"

The astounded George swung around to find Brian Rea, a good friend of his from years gone past. Standing beaming. His hand outstretched.

"Brian, we are just on our way home from holidays. We had a couple of weeks down near Donaghadee. It is good to see you," was the reply.

Hurriedly Brian continued, "I can't stop now, George. I am rushing to catch a lift here. But I will see you again sometime."

With that he dashed off.

The shop assistant was by now standing at George's elbow.

"Can I help you, sir?" she asked, looking down at the pair of training-shoes hanging loosely from his left hand.

Liz's eyes met those of her husband. It was more than a questioning look. It was a how-are-you-going-to-get-out-of-this-one? look.

How was he going to get out of this one?

"Yes, thank you," he replied. Ever so calmly. "We would like this pair of training-shoes."

He reached her whatever it was that Brian had just put into his hand. And he reached his wondering wife a pair of training-shoes for Aaron. In a carrier bag.

The assistant gave him three pounds change, which he used to top up the petrol in the Renault 5.

And they went on their way. Rejoicing.

God had provided for them and their little ones. As He had said He would.

And the promise did extend to training-shoes!

Fifteen years later, George and Liz were returning from holiday, again. The sailing had been delayed. So they had an hour to spend. It was frustrating. They were experiencing that when you're on your way home - feeling, you-can't-wait-to-be-home.

Since there wasn't much they could do about the situation,

they decided to take a walk up the town. As they stood there, gazing into that shop window in Stranraer, they were looking but not seeing. They were talking away to each other. Oblivious to the fact that there was nothing in the window but cereals. Stacks of various sizes, of packets of Cornflakes of various sizes.

"I hope you realise, love," Liz said, in the course of the conversation, "that we have no money left. And the kitchen cupboard will be empty when we get home."

"What are you telling me that for, Liz?" George replied, slightly surprised that his wife, who had become accustomed to the bountiful provision of their God, should even let that worry her.

"Sure you know as well as I do," he went on, "that we have never lacked anything in the past sixteen years."

"I know that," agreed Liz. "But I just thought that you would like to know how we stood."

It slowly registered with George that the window, in which they were both pretending to show such an intense interest, was filled with packets of Cornflakes. Dozens of them.

"Liz, do you know what I was just thinking?" he reflected. "If we had a packet of Cornflakes that had never run done, no matter how much had been used out of it, for sixteen years, it would be headline news in the papers. They would be talking about it every night on the television. People would be coming from as far away as America and Australia to see it. Yet your wee purse has never been empty in all those years. And nobody knows a single thing about it."

He ended, as he began. With a question. A different one this time.

"Isn't God wonderful?" he enquired.

Liz said no more.

She knew that God was wonderful. George was right.

When they arrived home, much later that evening, there was enough money in an envelope in the hall to replenish their larder.

Their Heavenly Father had proved His faithfulness, once more!

CHAPTER 31
The Ezra Project

God had another crying-out need to meet.

Not only for George, and his family. But for the whole fellowship in Randalstown.

It was for a new building.

The assembly had outgrown the little meeting-house that they had used. So many people crushed into it on a Sunday evening that they expected it to burst open. Explode. Like a chestnut popping on a hot coal fire.

They eventually had to remove a window. Merely to allow the thirty-or-so people sitting in the garden to hear what was being said inside.

Mr. Eric Stewart from Templemore Hall had been their speaker one evening. The theme of his message had been, "Fill up before the mountain."

This sign outside a petrol station had caught his attention. On his travels somewhere. It so struck his heart that he felt he should share it with the meeting.

"I feel that you have a mountain ahead," he had remarked, in the course of his address. "And you will need to be filled with the Spirit to conquer it."

Joe Bailie, Pat Kitchen and George knew, as overseers, what their mountain was. At that particular time.

Does God want us to build? Something bigger? Provide more facilities for the expansion of the work.

They had tried to interest others in the fellowship in going out to form a new church. But nobody seemed to want to leave.

Yet how could they build? They didn't believe in carrying

a massive bank balance. So they kept continually emptying the coffers. Giving away any money that they received, to the work of the Lord, as soon as it came in.

It was also their deep conviction that they should never make their requirements known publicly. God alone should know their needs. So there would be no appeals for money.

Add to that, the fact that it was their belief that they should owe no man anything. So debt was out.

No big credit balance. No public appeals. No debt.

How could a group like that build anything? Where would the money come from?

They only had thirty shillings in the Bank.

After discussing the possibility of re-building, often, and at some length, they decided to listen to one of their tapes of Willie Mullan's preaching. Perhaps God would guide them. Through His word.

"It's all right talking about having faith in God," was the challenge of the tape-message. "But can you trust Him when you have only thirty-bob in your pocket?"

God had spoken. To each individually. To all three as a group. They bowed their hearts before Him. Confident that He would lead the way.

Hence began "The Ezra Project," as they had code-named their operation.

They called upon the members of the church to pray and fast for ten days. Seeking a right way for them and their families. As Ezra had done in the Bible (Ezra 8 v 21).

Then they decided to build.

When they had needed one thousand pounds for supplies, to continue the building work, George was on his knees. In his living room. Desperately crying to God, who was to be the Only One to know of their needs.

As he pleaded with God, there was a knock on the back door. When George went to answer it, he found John Laughlin, from their fellowship, standing there.

He offered George a brown paper bag. "My father asked

me to give you that, George. It's for the building project," he explained.

When he opened the bag, George found that his prayers had been answered. While he had been in the process of asking. God had been arranging the solution.

The brown paper bag contained one thousand pounds. In banknotes.

What a relief!

But the next week it was three thousand pounds that they had to find. And still it came! Miraculously.

Many brought gifts of jewellery. Antiques. In fact anything they could get their hands on that could be turned into money. For the building work.

There were problems to be surmounted.

Planning permission...

There were mountains to be conquered.

Building control...

And every time they climbed to the top of one, apparently insurmountable peak, they saw another one. Even higher. Looming up in the misty-distance.

Five thousand pounds....

But they overlooked something as they gazed from peak to peak. From the summit of one mountain to the summit of the next.

It was that between every two mountain tops there lies a valley. And in the valley there was God. Waiting to guide them gently down the slopes of the mountain they had just climbed. And to lead them, sometimes breathless with fear, or exhausted by exertion, right up the tip of the next one!

Having completed the whole building enterprise with their own hands, the Christians had to be told to stop bringing money and materials. No more was required.

In the final analysis there had been enough-and-to-spare to finish the work.

Benefactors came from all walks of life. Far too numerous to mention.

An opening praise service was held on its completion. To

praise God for all His bounty. And to thank his servants for their sacrificial giving.

To rejoice in the brand-new much-bigger Meeting House. And to pray that non-Christians might come to know the Lord, and that Christians might come to know the Lord even better, within its walls.

The Ezra Project has lasted for almost two years. And had cost £65,000.

Yet they had operated according to their convictions. They hadn't ever built up a big credit balance in a Building Fund. Nor had they ever made a need known publicly. And they had never once been in debt!

God had poured out His manifold blessings to the full.

CHAPTER 32

Spreading The Word

George was kneeling alone in the Garden Tomb. Outside the walls of Jerusalem.

He was leading a party to the Holy Land. But he had to get away from them. To commune with God. For he had a problem. A burden on his soul.

It was concerning his testimony.

For many years now he had been speaking to people. In large groups and small. He had spoken to hundreds of people. Thousands. Telling them joyfully of the wonderful things that God had done in his life.

Recently, however, because of an incident that had taken place, through no fault of his own, he had become discouraged. A reticence had crept over his desire to tell his story abroad. Like a cold wave breaking over a rock. It chilled and washed away his original enthusiasm.

He wanted to be on fire again. Kneeling there he was pleading with God.

"Please God, give me the desire to tell my story to others again," he prayed. "I feel ashamed by my silence, after all that You have done for me. If it is Your will that I should do so, when I get home to Ulster will You please open the doors. And I will go through them. By Your grace I will tell them. I want to tell the world about Jesus.

I ask this in His Own Name. Amen."

Leaving the matter with God, he returned to his group. Who were waiting for him.

When he arrived back in Northern Ireland, Christian leaders began contacting him. Asking him to come to their Church or fellowship. To relate his experiences of God.

This was an answer to prayer. George responded in a positive way. He couldn't do anything else. Hadn't he promised his Heavenly Father that he would? In that lonely encounter in the tomb.

However, as he began to tell his life story afresh, he was often forced to conclude his remarks with the words, "There's far more than this that I could tell you. But the clock has beaten us once again. There just wouldn't be time."

The seventh invitation that he received, in this new round of Divinely arranged appointments, came from his friend Derick Bingham.

"George," he said one morning on the telephone. "We would like you to come to the Crescent Church in Belfast, some Tuesday evening. And tell your story. All of it. We don't want any of this, 'There's more that I could tell you but I just haven't the time,' stuff. We will give you as much time as you want. We want to hear the whole story. Everything. And we don't care how long it takes!"

So it was agreed.

George was to go to the Crescent Church, on Tuesday 18th December, 1979 to tell the story of his conversion.

And preservation.

And restoration.

And emancipation.

Derick had advertised the meeting as, "A Night With A Difference."

And that's exactly what it turned out to be.

The Tuesday night congregation had been warned that there was no time limit whatsoever being placed on this meeting. It was to be open-ended.

"You can bring a flask and a couple of sandwiches with you if you like," Derick had quipped.

Instead of putting the prospective audience off, this warning proved to have the opposite effect. The church was packed to capacity. Well before the service was due to commence. And they had come prepared for a long, long sit. To hear it all. Every bit of it.

And they did.

The atmosphere was impregnated by the presence of God. Nobody noticed when they had been sitting for two hours. They were riveted to their seats. Hanging on every word.

And the surge of spiritual charge that was generated in that meeting didn't throb and kick, then splutter and die, when the lights were put out, and the heat went off in the Crescent Church that night.

Through tape recordings of that testimony, in its entirety, it became a thrust of Divine Power. Penetrating to the ends of the earth. It brought a new radiance of light, to lives enshrouded in darkness. And it provided a fresh pulse of power to struggling, flickering flames of Christian witness.

The full extent of the response to that one single meeting, is still being metered in Heaven.

Souls have been saved. Backsliders restored. The people of God blessed. Buildings have been erected in Tanzania....

A publican, who was an atheist, found the Saviour. And sold his pub...

A truck driver was halted from stabbing his boss. In Canada. After listening to the tape in his cab. On the way to commit a murder...

Since that memorable night in December, 1979, George has been projected into the work of an evangelist. He has seen hundreds of souls led to Christ for salvation.

And has proved daily,

As all the years have passed.

And continues to prove daily,

As each new day goes past,

What he found out many years ago.

Dancing around a bedroom,

With his wife in his arms,

And Christ in his heart.

That,

"This is For Real!"

This Is For Real